PRIME TIME LIVING

A plan for getting more out of life as you grow older

Y0-BDO-706

DAVID WHITE WITH CHRISTY YINGLING

Pacific Press® Publishing Association
Nampa, Idaho
Oshawa, Ontario, Canada
www.pacificpress.com

Book design by Dennis Ferree
Photographer/Artist: Karan Kapoor/Getty Images

David White presents seminars on making the most of one's retirement years. To arrange for his services, contact the public rela-
tions director at Pacific Press, P.O. Box 5353, Nampa, ID 83653-
5353; telephone (208) 465-2500.

Library of Congress Cataloging-in-Publication Data

White, David, 1940 May 13–
Prime-time living/David White with Christy Yingling.
p. cm.
ISBN: 0-8163-2081-0
1. Retirement—United States. 2. Aging—United States. 3. Older
people—Health and hygiene—United States. I. Yingling,
Christy, 1978– II. Title.

HQ1063.2.U6W543 2005
646.7'9—dc22   2005043111

Additional copies of this book are available
by calling toll free 1-800-765-6955 or by visiting
http://www.adventistbookcenter.com.

Dedication

To my mother, Mary White Reay, ninety; my stepfather, Bryce Reay, ninety-eight; and my mother-in-law, Rhea Goodacre, ninety-two. And in memory of my dad, Benjamin White, who died in 1987 at seventy-one; and my father-in-law, William Goodacre, who died in 2004 at eighty-seven. Each of these significant persons provided inspiration for the writing of this book.

And to Harry Bennett, whose life and continuing ministry at ninety is the epitome of the principles of the prime-time living during retirement outlined in the pages of this book.

Table of Contents

Introduction

Congratulations! You are investing in your future. Retirement is an inevitable and important part of life. Yet, tragically, few people learn how to maximize this potentially wonderful time. Why? Perhaps some are distressed by the familiar quip, "Nothing is certain except death and taxes." Retirement is often equated with aging and eventual death. Because of that negative association, people avoid planning for the important later stages in life.

Medical knowledge and innovations have added years to the human life span. The number of people who fall into the upper age brackets has been gradually increasing. In the year 1900, the life expectancy at birth was 46.4 years for a male and 49 years for a female. In 2000, life expectancy at birth was 73.2 years for a male and 79.7 years for a female.[1] Just imagine—you can expect to live from twenty-seven to thirty-one years longer than someone born a century ago! And that's just the average; even centenarians are no longer rare. Willard Scott, weather reporter for NBC News' *Today* show, says "happy birthday" every week to twelve people who are one hundred or more. And Mr. Scott mentions only twelve each week because of time constraints; he receives hundreds of other requests.

As you venture into the unknown future, lay aside the stereotypical image of older people as feeble, frail, unhealthy, lonely, and depressed. As you see the possibilities for a productive, happy, healthy, rewarding life, you will realize that this is the beginning of your best years. That is what *Prime-Time Living* is all about.

Why read this book?

Why read a book about aging? Perhaps you feel it won't do any good; it's too late. Denial may enter in—"I'm not getting old." Fear may be another issue: Being old will come soon enough without worrying about it. In actuality, you spend approximately one-quarter of your life growing up and the remaining three-quarters growing old. Yet many have failed to focus on this significant period. How can these years be the best years of your life? *Prime-Time Living* will show how

- the retirement years can be healthy and productive.
- financial planning right now can alleviate financial stress as you become older.
- your prime-time years can be a time when you can focus more fully on relationships with your spouse, children, and grandchildren.
- you can enjoy this time with friends (both long-time and new).
- retirement can provide time for mental stimulation: through learning, acquiring new skills, and sharing wisdom.
- you can make a positive impact on your community.
- you can enjoy spiritual growth and fulfillment.

Primarily, this book is meant to help you stay healthy and enjoy quality living during your retirement years. More important than the number of years you live is the quality of those years. You are familiar with the term *life span*—how long a person may live. This book is more about *health span*. Scientific research shows that if you establish healthy habits, you can expect to add years to your life expectancy. If you follow the lifestyle habits outlined in this book, you can add years to your "health expectancy." I'm not worrying about how many more years I'll live. That's up to God. My focus is on adding some zest and purpose to life, thus improving the quality of the years ahead.

The best years are ahead

Aging poses many challenges. If you're experiencing midlife crisis, you may feel that you already have one foot in the grave. When you were younger, life was about looking and reaching forward—job promotions, rearing children, vacations. You were fulfilling dreams. All of a sudden, midlife enters the scene. Perhaps you're finding that your job is not as secure as you thought. Your children are in their teens and focused on their lives and their friends. You may feel a little tired and notice you're not bouncing back from physical exertion as rapidly as you used to. You may experience a few more aches and pains. Perhaps your blood pressure has increased slightly, and even the bathroom scale has begun to give you bad news. These changes may prompt some scary questions: "Is this all there is to life? Am I on the downside of the hill?"

Moses may have asked that same question. Take a look at him on his eightieth birthday. For the past forty years, he's been in the desert, herding sheep. He may well have been asking himself, "Why did I kill that Egyptian? How did I mess up my life so badly? Is this all I'm going to accomplish?"

Then God catches Moses' attention and says, "I want you to go to Egypt and talk to Pharaoh. I want you to lead my people out of Egypt."

Moses replies, "You've got to be kidding! I can't speak Egyptian anymore—it's been forty years." Moses is thinking he's over the hill. After all, he is eighty years old!

But God says, "Moses, the best years of your life are before you!"[2]

That's just the beginning of the story. At age eighty, Moses stands before Pharaoh and his advisors. Subsequently, he leads what were probably more than a million people out of Egypt. He talks with God at Sinai, receives the Ten Commandments, oversees the building of the tabernacle, and leads the children of Israel to the border of the Promised Land.

When Moses was eighty, he could easily have thought, *I should start gearing down. There isn't much left for me to do except look after these sheep a little longer and then die.* But God said, "Gear up, Moses. I have a plan for you." Most of what made Moses memorable occurred during the last third of his life—forty productive years.

Prime-time living is not about gearing down for retirement. It's about gearing up for what has the potential to be the most exciting period of your life!

---

1. Information about life expectancy from 1900 to 2000 from the Centers for Disease Control and Prevention: <http://www.cdc.gov/nchs/fastats/lifexpec.htm>.
2. Read the story in Exodus 2 and 3.

Overcoming the Myths of Aging[1]

Have you noticed aches and pains you didn't have a few years ago? Aging involves changes. In addition to the changes in your own life, you probably see changes in the lives of your friends. A close friend has a heart attack and dies. A parent dies. These events may cause you to re-examine your own health. Disturbing thoughts creep in: *Is this all there is to life? Am I past my prime?* Negative changes can lead to confusion, denial, depression, or anxiety. Before that happens a timeout may be helpful: a time to take stock of where you've been, where you are now, and where you want to be in the future. Even though some changes are inevitable, you can do many positive things to improve your life.

Now is the time for you to plan for a dynamic, fulfilling, and exhilarating life in the future. Whatever bad choices you may have made, you cannot relive the past or change those decisions. From this moment on, though, things can be different. God loves you and wants you to enjoy a good quality of life, to enjoy life to its utmost (see John 10:10). Regardless of where you find yourself at this moment—rich or poor, successful or failing, in good health or poor health—God accepts and loves you. He forgives you for your negative behaviors, even if you've been abusing your body with poor health choices. He has a plan for you now, a plan that includes a happy and dynamic future. Though you may think of yourself as over the hill, God doesn't think of you in that way. You can experience some of your most fulfilling years in your sixties, seventies, eighties, and, yes, even in your nineties. First, though, you must overcome some difficulties.

Aging can be difficult for many reasons. Two challenges older people face are ageism and the myths of aging. Ageism involves prejudices and stereotypes that distort society's view of older people simply because of their age. Many people, even those who are older, also have false ideas about what happens when you age. These false ideas are also known as the myths of aging.

Many of the terms used to refer to older people are not very positive. We hear things such as "old fogies," "senile," "crotchety," "grumpy old men," "out to pasture," and other derogatory epithets. In our society, growing older has acquired an undesirable connotation.

Negative stereotypes are not reserved only for those over sixty-five. Employers may resent the fact that a fifty-year-old employee costs them more than a twenty-five-year-old employee. The fifty-year-old receives more salary and more vacation pay. Consequently, they may want to fire that older employee. This is ageism. It is also discrimination.

Advertising is another major venue of ageism. Notice the age of most models. Very few have gray hair. And in advertisements, references to aging generally occur in the context of how to avoid it—they're selling wrinkle creams, face-lifts, and other products and procedures to prolong youth or the appearance of youthfulness. This is a more subtle form of ageism.

Myths of aging

Ageism arises from the myths about aging that are omnipresent in our society. There's an old story about a couple of young boys who had heard of an elderly sage's wisdom and wanted to trick him. As the boys approached the sage, one of them grasped a bird, hiding all but its tail feathers. Putting his hands behind his back, the boy asked, "Is the bird dead or alive?" If the sage replied, "The bird is alive," the boy would squeeze the life out of the bird. If the sage replied, "The bird is dead," the boy would release the bird, proving it to be alive. After a moment of thought, the sage answered the boy's question with these words: "Whether the bird is dead or alive is in your hands." Similarly, regarding the myths of aging, belief or disbelief is in your hands.

Many of the myths of aging contain elements of truth, and others are completely false. Some were thought to be true years ago, but as knowledge has increased, they've been disproved. And our increased knowledge has changed the very process of aging. However, many people still accept these myths as factual—including many older adults themselves. Unfortunately, that can, unnecessarily, turn myth into reality. Let's look at seven common myths about aging.

Myth #1: Older adults are a homogeneous group

What people mean is that older adults are all alike. But older adults are not as homogeneous a group as teenagers are, for example. People are teenagers for only seven years. It's not uncommon now for people to live to be one hundred. So, if we define "older adults" as people sixty-five years of age and older, this category covers thirty-five years. And this segment of the population is a very diverse group in age, health, and every other comparable facet of life.

Some seniors are couch potatoes, with little desire to be active. They have a poor quality of life. However, most older adults are healthy and enjoy an excellent quality of life. They travel and are active in their communities and churches. They have many friends and are engaged in life. Many say, "This is the greatest time of my life." Because of the huge differences among older people, it's unfair to generalize about them. The truth is that the longer people live, the more diverse they become.

Myth #2: To be old is to be sick

Of course older people get sick. So do younger people! The question is: Are the thirty-five million Americans who are sixty-five years of age and older a group of sick people? The answer is No! While some older people are sick, many are in good health. In a study of 67,469 people between the ages of sixty-five and seventy-four conducted by the Center for Disease Control and Prevention, 74.5 percent reported their health as "good to excellent."

Just observe individuals in their upper eighties and nineties and notice how many are healthy. I interviewed many individuals in that particular age group and was surprised at the level of health they were enjoying—not only physical health, but also emotional, social, intellectual, and spiritual health.

Mary Ann is an example of an older adult who is very healthy. She is ninety-three going on nineteen. A widow of twenty years, she lives alone in a senior condominium community. She claims she is never bored. She still does volunteer work as a nurse every other week. And she sews for those who can't do it for themselves.

I attended a Friday evening vesper program in which Mary Ann led out in an enthusiastic song service. After the program, she excitedly told me about her recent cruise to the Bahamas with her family. Mary Ann is nothing like the sixty-five-year-old couch potato who always complains about aches and pains. She says her knee "hurts a little," but she jumps up and says, "See? I can still get out of my chair without holding on to something!"

There is a difference between age-related changes and risk factors. Mary Ann's knee pain is probably an age-related change. Age-related changes are changes related to growing older that cannot be reversed. The older person needs to compensate for these changes. I'm not a young adult any longer; I shouldn't expect to have the looks, endurance, or strength of a young adult. I need to learn to enjoy the maturity and wisdom of a sixty-four-year-old.

People can change risk factors, however. If I suffer fatigue because I'm forty to fifty pounds overweight, that extra weight is a risk factor. I need to lose weight, engage in regular exercise, make wiser food choices, obtain proper rest, and control the stress level in my life. Because of my choices, the fatigue will be diminished or eradicated, and I'll feel stronger and more energized.

The myth "to be old is to be sick" has a very unfortunate consequence. Treatable conditions may go untreated simply because the person experiencing it, the family, or even the medical staff expects problems with age and so considers it normal. If a condition or problem is treatable, it should be treated whether the person experiencing it is young or old. That person has a right to enjoy life to the fullest extent possible.

Whether or not you are healthy lies in your hands. Choose to live healthfully and enjoy life.

Myth #3: Older people are isolated and lonely

Isolation and loneliness have nothing to do with age. While it is true that some old people are isolated and lonely, there are also young people who are isolated and lonely. Many older people have a wonderful network of friends and contacts. One of the most important factors in healthy aging is staying engaged in life. Mary Ann is a prime example of that. She asks, "How can I be lonely? I have hundreds of friends." And she isn't exaggerating. She is neither isolated nor lonely.

Ted, a seventy-five-year-old, is a retired academy principal. He and his wife deliver Meals on Wheels one day a week. Ted also teaches a Bible class each week in his church. He says, "I stay active, and I'm not going to let that change."

Other individuals in the retirement community where Mary Ann lives choose to isolate themselves from their neighbors. The story is told of one man who moved into the community. He asked his neighbor if the people in the community were friendly. The neighbor replied with a question: "What were your neighbors like where you lived before?"

The man replied, "They were very unfriendly and sometimes mean."

To this the neighbor answered, "You will probably find the people in this community the same."

I expect that if the new guy on the block had answered, "The people were all very friendly," the neighbor's reply would have followed suit: "You will find the people here the same—very friendly." People who are friendly and try to reach out to others find that their neighbors respond in like manner.

Retirement provides you the opportunity to involve yourself even more deeply in your community and church. The choice to isolate yourself and withdraw from people or to expand your social involvement is in your hands. Is the social involvement "bird" in your hand dead or alive?

Myth #4: Older people don't pull their weight

Many economists and government leaders look at the thirty-five million people sixty-five years of age and older drawing Social Security and conclude: "These people are a drain on our economy." This myth may arise from the fact that most of these people are not working at a paycheck-producing job. Unfortunately, many older people themselves accept this idea as a fact rather than a myth.

Recall that we said a myth sometimes has some truth mixed in with the error. People over sixty-five do draw Social Security. And most of those over sixty-five do not work at a full-time, paying job. The problem lies in not looking at all the contributions older Americans make.

Older Americans are not a drain on society either financially or in service to the community. They spend a lot of money on goods and services. Media advertisers target seniors because they recognize the importance of this segment of the market. In addition to boosting the economy through spending, many older people also take the time to volunteer, becoming a valuable community resource.

Can seniors become a burden to their family and to society? Yes, of course. However, seniors today, as never before, can make a significant contribution to society. They're healthier, live longer, and are more mobile than the seniors of previous generations.

The prevalent philosophy today is "live and let live." In other words, you do your thing; I'll do mine—you're on your own! We need to change that concept to a new one: "Live and help live." Proverbs 11:25 says, "A generous man will prosper; he who refreshes others will himself be refreshed." When you reach out and help someone else, you are the one truly blessed. Jesus Himself said, "It is more blessed to give than to receive" (Acts 20:35).

Myth #5: Aging brings an inevitable decline in intellectual abilities

The truth that contradicts this myth is so important that I've devoted a whole chapter to intellectual health. Recent research indicates that healthy older adults show only a slight decline in cognitive skills, and most receive an increase in wisdom due to a lifetime of experience.

One of the greatest joys in life is learning new things. Retired people can have a greater opportunity to experience this joy because of the increase of their free time. One of my personal goals is to take some continuing education classes. There are so many wonderful things to learn, and all it takes is a little curiosity and some time and effort.

Older adults are just as capable of learning as are younger individuals. Some find it harder simply because their brains have become rusty through disuse. Your mind is a wonderful gift. Keep using it so that you don't lose it.

Myth #6: Older people are depressed

Emotional health is a concern for everyone, no matter what his or her stage in life. This myth is another example of truth mixed with error. Some older people are indeed depressed. However, depression is a treatable condition. Simple lifestyle habits can greatly reduce or even eliminate feelings of depression.[2] And for tougher cases, doctors can provide effective help. One of our goals should be to exhibit and enjoy a happy spirit, not a depressed one. (Chapter 8 will cover emotional health in more depth.)

Myth #7: Older people are set in their ways; either they will not change or it is too late for them to change

Habits do become deeply ingrained with the passing of time. However, it is never too late for people to make lifestyle changes and thereby enjoy better health of all kinds. Again, as in the story of the sage, the boys, and the bird, it's in our hands.

Older adults can reap great benefits from making positive changes in lifestyle. One example of this is the matter of exercise. When people start to exercise—especially a moderate walking program based on ability—they often begin to feel better almost immediately. Of course, you should check with your physician before you begin an exercise program. Your physician can provide you with advice regarding the intensity and duration that will fit your particular health needs.

Societal myths lead to personal assumptions

The myths we have looked at are stereotypes that society believes about senior citizens. Each of us has to decide whether to accept or reject these stereotypes. That choice can be called a personal assumption. And the assumptions to which we subscribe—positive and negative—determine our behavior. What do I mean? Here's an example: Myth # 7 says, "Older people are set in their ways; either they will not change, or it is too late for them to change." If I assume that it's too late to change my lifestyle, I won't change my behavior. If I assume that it *isn't* too late to make a difference in my health, I *can* change my behavior. There's no roadblock to making that change happen.

Allow me to give you an illustration of this principle. I have a friend who shared with me his weight struggles. Based on his height of five feet, eleven inches, the upper limit of his weight should be 175 pounds. Recently his weight went up to 179 pounds. The self-talk started right away. "Metabolism slows down when people get older. It's just a fact of life. It's OK. I'm only four pounds overweight." Then his weight increased to 185 pounds. That voice in his head kicked in again: "It's OK. I'm only ten pounds overweight." He subscribed to the societal myth about aging and metabolism, and that led to his personal assumption that it didn't matter; it was simply an inevitable change. He rationalized that such a small amount of weight on the chart wouldn't really make a difference anyway.

With such an assumption, what was his behavior? You're right. It remained the same. He made no change in his eating habits and no change in his exercise habits. He wasn't concerned about his weight.

When, several months later, this man stepped on the scale, it read 189 pounds. This time his assumption changed. The new assumption was, "One hundred eighty-nine pounds is not acceptable." When he changed his assumption, his behavior began to change. He adopted new eating and exercising habits. As a result, over the next five months his weight dropped to 165 pounds. He now looks and feels better.

Invalid assumptions (A) determine unhealthy behavior (B), which leads to consequences (C). Those consequences can lead to disabilities and/or premature death (D). Graphically, it looks like this:

$$A_{ssumptions} \rightarrow B_{ehavior} \rightarrow C_{onsequences} \rightarrow D_{eath}$$

Accepting false personal assumptions can cause you to end up in a downward spiral. My friend knows that the consequences of being overweight are bad. He realized that he was facing the threat of disabilities, diabetes, heart disease, certain types of cancers, a lesser quality of life, and lower feelings of self-worth. He didn't want to experience the consequences of being overweight, so he changed his assumption, which in turn changed his behavior. It wasn't too late for him, nor is it too late for you.

Myths are like old fables. They're outdated and out of touch with reality. But they'll have no effect on you unless you allow them to become a part of your thinking and your assumptions. Then they can affect your behavior and your life. Think about how your assumptions affect your behavior.

HOMEWORK:
1. List the ways ageism has affected you.
2. Regarding myth # 4:
    (b)List the ways you are contributing to your family or community.
    (c)List things you would consider doing to contribute to your community. (For some ideas, see chapter 9, "Social Health.")
3. List one or two assumptions you have concerning your health that affect your behaviors and your health.

---

1. John W. Rowe and Robert L. Kahn list several myths of aging—two of which I have borrowed—in their book *Successful Aging* (New York: Pantheon, 1998). Their book is excellent, well worth reading.

2. The suggestions in this book are not intended to cure clinical depression. If you are depressed for more than a two-week period, see a health-care professional.

CHAPTER 2

Prime-Time Aging

Ben, a retired electrician and part-time dairy farmer, was a hardworking, loving father of two sons. Unfortunately, Ben started smoking in his late teens, and it soon became a habit he couldn't break until late in life. In his sixties he developed a heart condition. When he was seventy-one, he had a massive heart attack and died instantly. This is normal aging, a less than ideal lifestyle that can lead to diseases, disability, decline, and early death.

Bryce, ninety-eight, is thoroughly enjoying life. He lives in a retirement condominium with his wife, who is ninety. Together they work a large garden and walk more than half a mile daily, and Bryce does eight minutes of stretching and squats daily. Intellectually, he is very sharp. He reads the *Reader's Digest* and *National Geographic* and keeps up with current events by watching the evening news. Bryce's daily schedule includes time for devotions and prayer. He is an active deacon in his church, drives his car on short trips, and continues to manage his own finances. At ninety-eight, Bryce has no known health problems and takes virtually no prescription medications. His doctor, finding nothing wrong with him at his last checkup, could say only, "Come back in six months!" Bryce is the epitome of prime-time aging.

I know Ben's story well. He was my dad. Dad did a lot of things right. Many aspects of his lifestyle were good, but the smoking habit caused major health problems. I also know Bryce very well.

He's my stepdad. In these two men, I've witnessed firsthand the effects of normal aging and prime-time aging. I know which one I want to experience.

Normal aging versus prime-time aging

Nowadays, most people consider normal aging to mean higher-than-ideal blood pressure and weight, a loss of muscle tissue, and so forth. After all, when the nurse at the doctor's office takes your blood pressure, you probably ask, "How is it?" and she replies, "For someone your age, it's good." And when you have blood work done and you ask, "How's my cholesterol and sugar?" again the reply is, "For your age, it's OK." And your increasing weight is "OK for your age," and so it goes.

In our society, people accept and even expect that normal aging means increased blood pressure and weight, higher blood levels of sugar and cholesterol, and declining strength. This normal aging leads to "normal" diseases, "normal" medications, "normal" disabilities, and finally, a "normal" death.

Look at the figure below that depicts normal aging. Notice the gradual decline. Normal aging consists of experiencing *signs*—the body's form of road signs that warn you of the dangers ahead—followed by *symptoms* (physical signals that something is wrong in your body), then *disease, disability,* and finally *death*.

The Typical Decline

"Normal aging"
> **Signs**
>> **Symptoms**
>>> **Disease**
>>>> **Disability**
>>>>> **Death**

Let's look at the factors that lead to this decline, using Sam as our example.

"Normal aging": Sam's normal aging begins with the typical American lifestyle of poor health habits: His diet is comprised largely of fast-food meals and other foods high in saturated fat and highly

refined carbohydrates, like rich desserts. He has a high-stress lifestyle. And he does little or no exercise of enough intensity to benefit him. These things take a toll on his health.

Signs: The signs of normal aging started early in Sam's life. The numbers on the bathroom scale indicated he was just a little over the desirable body weight. Oh, he thought, it's not enough to get concerned about. Then he noticed that he became a little winded when he climbed a flight of stairs, and his blood cholesterol level was a little high. Each of these is a sign that should have alerted Sam to a potential problem. But since no bells, whistles, or sirens sounded warnings, Sam continued on the same course, hoping that things would get better by themselves. He thought, I don't need to do anything drastic—after all, I'm still young.

Symptoms: The signs became more insistent; now they were symptoms. Sam's blood pressure rose, and so did his blood sugar level. Occasionally, he felt a little pain around his heart when he exerted himself. And the weight problem? Well, he told himself, many people are worse than I am. It happens to many people my age.

At this point the bells, whistles, and sirens are sounding. Sam knew they were sounding, but he found it too easy to ignore the warnings and go on with his busy life.

Disease/Illness: When Sam ignored the signs and symptoms, disease was the inevitable result. In his case, it was heart disease complicated by diabetes. Other people suffer heart attacks, lung cancer, hypertension, chronic obstructive pulmonary disease (COPD), or liver disease. Many of the diseases people suffer are what we call lifestyle diseases—meaning diseases that people bring on by making poor lifestyle choices. Too many people assume that medications and a physician's care alone will restore them to a previous level of health.

Disability: Sam now found that he could no longer do many of the things that he once enjoyed. And he had to spend a considerable portion of his time treating his diseases. Disability means that to some extent people become dependent on someone else for their care, perhaps necessitating a move to a health-care facility. Disability significantly lowers quality of life.

However, contrary to popular belief, in many instances it's poor lifestyle rather than age that causes disability. The good news is that people can avoid the disabilities caused by wrong lifestyle choices. The key to reducing the risk of disability as you age lies in the prevention and treatment of chronic diseases such as high blood pressure and arthritis. "It is imperative that we start to explore ways of reducing disabled life expectancy and maximizing active life expectancy in old age."[1]

Death: Sam died when he was sixty-nine, when many people are still active and enjoying their retirement. "Normal"—that is, premature—death is the last step in normal aging. In other words, people die earlier than they would have if they'd taken better care of themselves. Part of the problem is that many fail to take responsibility for their health. They rely on someone else (doctor, spouse, child) or something else (hospital, insurance company, medications) to keep them healthy.

Aging "normally" is easy. People don't need to make any effort or commitment. Nothing is required—not even their motivation. Many people are on the fast track to normal aging. Are you one of them?

Prime-time aging

During the past century, most retirees experienced normal aging. We don't have to anymore. It's obsolete, and it's time that we toss it out. Now we have a second option: prime-time aging. This option takes people one step at a time to better health. Of course, I'm not suggesting that we can eliminate death. Rather, I'm pointing out that by our choices we can delay or even eliminate the typically negative conditions perceived as normal aging. A great person once said, "The way we live determines how we die." I believe we need to adopt a new paradigm and picture aging as a positive experience—that of prime-time aging. Look at the model below.

Prime-Time Aging

Experience prime-time aging
Enjoy prime-time living
Make changes
Gear up and set goals

A hundred years ago, a man's life expectancy was around forty-five years and a woman's around fifty. For many, retirement was nonexistent. In years past, many people simply slid into retirement, giving it little thought or planning. They simply hoped they would stay healthy and that their finances would outlast them.

It's time for a change. It's time to make prime-time living choices so you can experience prime-time aging. It's time to trade in a lax, *laissez-faire* attitude for a planned and proactive approach to retirement. Let's develop a strategy to achieve a dynamic, rewarding, healthy retirement.

Our starting point will be to look at the five pillars that support the concept of prime-time aging. These are pillars of your entire being. They are the physical, intellectual, emotional, social, and spiritual aspects of life. In addition to these five pillars, we will consider another issue closely associated with retirement: financial health and planning.

The two main goals for prime-time living are (1) to make retirement the most rewarding time of your life and (2) to maximize quality in each of the above listed aspects of life. Today, the only aspect most people plan for in their retirement is their financial future. If they happen to go a step further, it is usually to ask, "Where are we going to live?" This is about as far as most people get. Let's look at the other aspects that make us human beings and that also deserve attention.

Spiritual: In normal aging, people's spiritual life may become very weak. They may expect that their involvement in church will decrease. They may stop reading all spiritual literature—even the Bible. Homebound people may lose interest in spiritual matters if they no longer have a vital connection with their church family.

So, in the spiritual realm, normal aging can lead to spiritual illness and even spiritual death. What a tragedy! Don't allow this to happen to you. Spiritual health provides a foundation for each of the other aspects of prime-time aging. Strong spiritual health provides meaning and purpose for life. You certainly don't want to retire your spiritual side, your relationship with Christ. Instead, your spiritual life can become even stronger as you age.

So, get ready for the greatest spiritual feast of your life! Set goals for spiritual growth. Decide what you want to accomplish in your personal being, in your church life, and in your sharing of blessings with others. Pray, and God will help you formulate a meaningful spiritual plan. Prime-time aging is a growing, inspiring, and spiritually healthy life.

Physical: Physical concerns may be what people think of second when they are nearing retirement—second after money. Normal aging leads to rapid physical decline. Prime-time aging means you don't have to accept what others say is the inevitable decline of your body. You continually look for new ways to make your body healthier—by eating plenty of fresh fruits and vegetables, avoiding bad fats, getting vitamin "S" (sunshine), and exercising as much as you and your physician feel comfortable with.

Physically, prime-time aging means avoiding disease as long as possible. Individuals who live to be one hundred have either been fortunate or were simply wise enough to make good lifestyle choices that have allowed them to avoid disease most or all their lives. Bryce, whom I mentioned at the beginning of this chapter, is an example of this. He spent his first and only night in a hospital at age ninety-six because of a fall. He has been fortunate and has also made wise health decisions. He is not an anomaly. Nearly all those who live into their late nineties have been able to avoid disease.

Prime-time aging is about developing strategies to maximize your genetic strengths or to compensate to the very best of your ability for poor genetics passed on to you. Genetics accounts for only about 30 percent of your health. To achieve physical prime-time aging, you must follow a comprehensive plan that includes a healthy yet enjoyable diet, a physically active lifestyle, adequate rest, water, sunshine, and fresh air. There are ninety-year-olds who ride across Europe on bicycles. If they can do it, so can you!

Financial: An important component of enjoying a successful retirement is having adequate funds. Financial health means living comfortably in the lifestyle to which you are accustomed. It should also mean having funds for the travel or entertainment you want. Poor financial health may mean not having the money to pay for unexpected bills or unanticipated health-care costs, not having the money to cover the necessities of living, or not having a few dollars for the extras in life that you may desire.

Two aspects comprise financial prime-time aging: (1) having acquired adequate funds to live comfortably, and (2) maximizing retirement dollars with sensible living. For many, the latter means living frugally, yet not financially impaired. You can learn to enjoy a lot of living on a few dollars.

Intellectual: Normal aging puts the brain into neutral to coast downhill. Prime-time aging gears the mind up for great intellectual quality of life in retirement. No one wants to give up brainpower after retiring, yet few think about how to preserve intellectual health during that phase of life. Part of the prime-time living strategy must involve developing and following a plan to stay intellectually healthy and not allow the mind to deteriorate or get ill. You must form a plan to keep your brain stimulated. Retirement gives you the opportunity to expand your intellectual horizons.

Emotional: Emotional health is another pillar of prime-time aging. Happiness is perhaps one of the most desired emotions—and one of the most elusive. You should not take it, or other constituents of emotional health, for granted.

Emotional health includes the ability to love and receive love from family and friends. Healthy emotional prime-time aging will bring ten, twenty, or thirty years of dynamic, happy, and peaceful life. Just as you aim to avoid physical disease, so, when it comes to mental health, you should strive to avoid emotional dysfunction.

Social: Prime-time aging also includes good social health. That means staying engaged with people, activities in the community, and in life itself. One important determinant of people's total health is the extent of their engagement with family and friends.

Socially, normal aging involves pulling back from people and avoiding social activities you enjoyed earlier in life. Just as poor health in the other areas can negatively affect your quality of life, so can poor social health. Prime-time aging, on the other hand, means maximizing your social potential. Whatever your temperament— whether you're shy or outgoing—try to go a little outside your comfort zone to reach out to others socially. Prime-time aging means planning to stay socially engaged and focused on the importance of people.

Prime-time aging means planning for your retirement in all areas of life. Don't leave any area to chance. That will result in normal aging. Prime-time aging doesn't just happen. You have to make it happen by thoughtful planning and by executing those plans. Take the first step by deciding what you want to accomplish in each of the six areas outlined above. This will be part of your homework, so start thinking about it now. If you do all the homework sections, by the time you finish this book, you'll have your own personalized prime-time aging plan.

Changes

Reaching your prime-time aging goals will involve making some changes in your life. Changing life habits takes time and effort. It's one of the most difficult things that people attempt to do. That's why most New Year's resolutions fail so quickly. By definition, habits are actions that people do on a regular basis. They are mind-body responses to life situations. Your daily routine is made up of a myriad of habits.

Most of these choices, good or bad, are the result of habits. To make changes in your life, you need to examine your attitudes, your assumptions, and your habits. You need a positive, "can do" attitude and a willingness to make whatever changes are necessary, no matter how difficult they may be.

In the story of the woman at the well recorded in John 4:1-43, Jesus used the classic sequence for motivating people to make a change in their life. Let's look at that story.

The first step is *attention*. In the story, Jesus caught the woman's attention by a simple request, "Will you give me a drink?" (verse 7). Something has already caught your attention. Perhaps you've noticed your blood pressure rising or you've been thinking about your retirement. Perhaps it was simply the title of this book.

Attention by itself is not enough to effect change. It must deepen into *interest*. Jesus sparked an interest in the Samaritan woman's mind when He offered her "living water" (verse 10). She wanted to know more about living water. The fact that you're reading this book shows that you're interested in having a dynamic, healthy retirement.

The third step is *desire*. Jesus proceeded to tell the Samaritan woman about living water. He told her that she would never thirst if she drank this living water. She responded, "Sir, give me this water so that I won't get thirsty and have to keep coming here to draw water" (verse 15). She wanted to drink water that would quench her thirst forever. You've been reading about the advantages of prime-time aging versus normal aging, and you know that God wants you to have this abundant life (John 10:10). God wants you to respond with the words of Psalm 40:8, "I desire to do your will, O God." When God's desires become your desires, change *will* happen. Pray and ask God that His desires for your life will become your desires.

The fourth step is *conviction*. Jesus brought conviction for change by pointing out the woman's sin and revealing that He is the Messiah (John 4:16-26). Do you know anyone like this woman—anyone who says, "It's my business how I eat, how I exercise, how I waste my brain, how I get angry"? Maybe that hits close to home. Conviction means you are convinced that a change must take place. When Peter preached a sermon to three thousand people on Pentecost, the Bible tells us, "They were cut to the heart and said . . . 'Brothers, what shall we do?' " (Acts 2:37). And when Jesus spoke to Paul, he became convinced that he must make a change in his life (see Acts 9:5, 6). You must be convinced that prime-time aging is worth the effort, and that you don't want normal aging, normal disability, and normal death.

Five frogs were sitting on a rock by a pond. One decided he was going to jump into the pond. How many frogs were left on the rock? Five—because deciding to do something and actually doing it are two different things! As important as conviction is, change won't happen without one final step: *action*. When the Samaritan woman decided to accept Jesus as her Savior, she acted on her decision. "The woman went back to the town and said to the people, 'Come, see a man who told me everything I ever did. Could this be the Christ?' " (John 10:28, 29). Change will take place in your life when you act upon your decision to experience prime-time aging.

Some people want the benefits of prime-time aging without having to change. That's why so many people suffer the consequences of normal aging. They lack the motivation necessary to start taking steps toward change. If you face this difficulty, you may need to pray that God will give you the necessary motivation. He motivated the woman at the well. He motivated Paul to change his behavior. He wants to motivate you too. He has promised, "Ask and it will be given to you" (Matthew 7:7). Trying to make a change without God's help leads only to frustration and failure. Allow God to help you. He's in the business of changing lives. He'll help you move from normal aging to prime-time aging.

Prime-time living

What is the action step that moves you toward prime-time aging? It is the matter of making choices in your daily living—prime-time living. Rather than merely talking the healthy talk, you walk the healthy walk. And here's an encouraging thought: It's unlikely that you've been doing everything wrong. No doubt, some of your lifestyle habits are good. If you want to change tracks from normal aging to prime-time aging, keep the good things you're doing and work on changing some of those bad habits. When you do so, you'll enjoy the benefits of physical, intellectual, emotional, social, financial, and spiritual health because you are acting on positive choices. You are proactive. You're drawing up a plan and making some significant changes.

Prime-time living doesn't guarantee a pain-free, disease-free, or disability-free life. However, it does give you a much better chance to achieve prime-time aging. At sixty-four, I look forward to thirty or more years of life. It is possible to be like Bryce and live disease-free until the age of ninety-eight. It is my goal to postpone both acute and chronic disease as long as possible. Through prime-time living, it certainly is possible to add ten to thirty years of quality life instead of experiencing the rapid deterioration of normal aging.

I first visited Charles when he was ninety-nine years young. He was living in his own home and was totally independent. He cooked his own meals—from "scratch," I might add. He informed me he didn't like "those TV dinners that aren't healthy for me." He said he loved spinach and obtained sufficient protein from the cottage cheese he ate. He ate no junk food. He showed me the large adult tricycle he rode for fifteen to twenty minutes a day.

I had the privilege of attending a party celebrating Charles's one-hundredth birthday. His church hosted it after the worship hour. He was still intellectually sharp, physically active, and socially and spiritually engaged in life. Charles was experiencing both quantity and quality of life.

Charles's life ended just a few weeks after he turned one hundred. He suffered from a fall and died shortly thereafter. What a life he lived! His was not a life of normal aging. It was the epitome of prime-time living and prime-time aging.

HOMEWORK:
1. Using the chart at the end of chapter 10, write down your health history and what you want to enjoy and accomplish in the future. Use a separate sheet of paper so you'll have enough room. (That should complete the first two horizontal columns in the chart.)
2. Do you know someone who is experiencing prime-time aging? What kinds of prime-time living decisions are they making?

---

1. Suzanne G. Leveille, Jack M. Guralnik, Luigi Ferrucci, and Jean A. Langlois, "Aging Successfully Until Death in Old Age: Opportunities for Increasing Active Life Expectancy," *American Journal of Epidemiology* 149, no. 7 (1999).

CHAPTER 3

Spiritual Health

An ancient myth tells of a magical fountain that gave eternal life to those who drank its water. Juan Ponce de León and many others searched in vain for that fountain. They hoped to stay healthy, maintain happiness, and live forever.

People still look for the fountain of youth. But most look in all the wrong places. The only solution to life's problems is the living water that God supplies. Jesus explained this concept to the woman at the well in Samaria, "Whoever drinks the water I give him will never thirst. Indeed, the water I give him will become in him a spring of water welling up to eternal life" (John 4:14). Some people miss the blessings they could receive because they eliminate the spiritual element from their lives. Others relegate spirituality to one day a week. Still others never quite integrate the living water into their daily lives to experience the full blessing of prime-time living.

The spiritual aspect of health is not simply "in addition to" all the other aspects. It is the foundation for living a healthy life. Even if you are strong in the other areas of health, without spiritual health, you cannot be whole. But if you are spiritually healthy, the benefits will spill over to the other areas of health. Compared to people with poor spiritual health, those with good spiritual health:

- have longer life expectancy
- have greater well-being and life satisfaction

- deal better with illness
- have fewer hospitalizations and shorter hospital stays
- suffer less anxiety and depression
- enjoy better immune system function.[1]

Religion or spirituality?

Religion and *spirituality* are not synonyms. They're interrelated, but we need to understand how they differ. *Spirituality* refers to people's belief in and connection with God. *Religion* refers to their connection to a church and its teachings and practices. Spirituality is the broad experience: people's personal experience with God. Religion is the practical expression of people's spirituality—their church experience and fellowship with other Christians. Both the experience and the expression of spirituality are important to maintaining good spiritual health.

The first and most basic part of spirituality is one's picture of God. What is He like? Do you trust Him? How do you interact with Him? These are all questions you should examine on your spiritual walk. If you have a false picture of God, you may not want Him in your life. If you think of Him as vengeful and harsh, you probably don't want to interact with Him or ask Him for help with your decisions.

It's not hard to keep God out of your life; He never forces His will on anyone. You can control your life. You can make life decisions based on your own version of a humanistic philosophy. If you don't want God to enter your decision-making process, He won't.

Christ

When you exclude Christ from your life, self is on the throne and life is chaotic.

There is a downside. Your life will be constantly chaotic—whether the chaos is internal or external. The diagram here shows this scenario. The result is spiritual atrophy.

Or you may choose to give God a minor role in your life. You may allow Him to enter into certain parts of your life, but keep self on the throne, making the decisions. You rely on your own knowledge, strength, and beliefs to make all of your decisions and to find happiness and quality of life. You believe God exists, but you don't trust Him with your life. You may even join a church and practice the parts of "religion" that fit your lifestyle. Whether or not you actually say the words, your prayer is, "God, stay in my life, but stay out of the way. I'm running the show. If I really mess up, I may need You to help me." If this is the case, you have a degree of spiritual health, but it's weak and sickly. Eventually you may die spiritually.

When you invite Christ in but stay on the throne, life is still tough.

As a third alternative, you may allow God to sit on the throne of your life. You may give Him control because you want Him to have it. You've asked Him to come into your life and to stay there. You believe in Him, trust Him with your life, and have a daily relationship with Him.

Yielding the throne of your life to Christ results in a peaceful, well-ordered life.

If your spiritual life matches this third diagram, you are spiritually healthy. You believe in yourself and the value God has given you, but you consider God more important than self. You base your decisions on God's will and His values. That makes sense. God knows what is best for you because He created you. He knows the best foods for you to eat. He knows the proper balance of work, exercise, and rest. His way leads to good emotional and intellectual health. Human ways—those in the first two throne diagrams—lead to hate, uncontrolled anger, selfishness, anxiety, and depression. God's way brings peace, purpose, and fulfillment to life. When you ask God to sit on the throne of your life, He gives you the fruit of the Spirit: love, joy, peace, patience, kindness, goodness, faithfulness, gentleness, and self-control (see Galatians 5:22, 23).

Spirituality and aging

Great news! You never have to worry that aging will diminish your spiritual health. That's because you can choose to keep growing spiritually no matter what your age. If you so choose, you can continue growing spiritually healthier for an eternity—starting right now and continuing in heaven. You may not be rich. You may wish you had just a little more brain power. You may have aches and pains. But spiritually, there are no limits. Our Friend God owns the universe, and He can't wait to share what He has. It doesn't matter how old you are. You can still participate in His exciting plan for your life. Psalm 92:12, 14 says, "The righteous will flourish like a palm tree, they will grow like a cedar of Lebanon. . . . They will still bear fruit in old age."

Do you want more wisdom? Here's a wonderful promise: "If any of you lacks wisdom, he should ask God, who gives generously to all without finding fault, and it will be given to him" (James 1:5). What a promise for us as we are growing older! We don't have to run out of wisdom. God is an all-wise God, and He'll share His wisdom with us.

How strong is your faith? The more you experience God's leading, the more you'll be able to trust Him. And trusting God will enable you to face the challenges of growing older. You won't have to worry about your life. God will take care of everything. Jesus said,

"Why do you worry about clothes? See how the lilies of the field grow. They do not labor or spin. Yet I tell you that not even Solomon in all his splendor was dressed like one of these. If that is how God clothes the grass of the field, which is here today and tomorrow is thrown into the fire, will he not much more clothe you?" (Matthew 6:28–30).

Jack, eighty-seven, and his wife, Gerry, seventy-nine, are both actively enjoying their retirement. Jack enjoys playing eighteen holes of golf whenever he can. Gerry enjoys oil painting and taking care of her flower garden. Both are active in their local Presbyterian church. Jack has been an elder at the church for fifty years. He still attends prayer breakfast every Tuesday. Both confirm that their spiritual health contributes to their quality of life. They both rate their happiness a ten on a ten-point scale. Jack says that being involved in church "gets me through my aches of arthritis."

Perhaps you're saying, "I'm not Jack. I don't understand what being a Christian or trusting God is like." Perhaps you had religion pushed on you as a child. Perhaps you had a bad experience as an adult in a church. Maybe you belonged to a church but didn't take time for God or the church. If so, you may feel it's too late for you to enjoy the benefits of being a Christian. Good news—it isn't too late! You can come to God no matter what your age. He is waiting with open arms.

When I was a hospital chaplain, I went into the chapel one morning. There in the open Bible was a piece of paper on which someone had scrawled the words, "Dear God, I am so sorry." Nothing else. No name; no story. Thinking that maybe whoever wrote those words would come back, I wrote a response at the bottom of the paper: "God said it's OK. He forgives you."

God says the same thing to you today: "It's OK. I forgive you." He's in the business of forgiving people. Jesus said, "Whoever comes to me I will never drive away" (John 6:37). This means that regardless of your background, your age, or your weaknesses, Jesus accepts you. When you come to Him, He will accept you. He will not turn you away.

He also said, "God so loved the world, that he gave his only begotten Son, that whosoever believeth in him should not perish, but have everlasting life" (John 3:16, KJV). God's offer to you of eternal life is based on His love for you. He loves you more than you can love even your own children. He has a great investment in you—He created you, and His Son, Jesus, died to save you. The return He receives for that sacrifice is your acceptance of His gift; He wants to spend an eternity with you. There are no strings attached. No hidden clauses. No timeshare to buy. God has paid for it. His offer is the offer of a lifetime, with benefits throughout your life on earth and for all eternity.

How do you accept this offer? It's very simple. Just tell God you want to accept it. You want Jesus to come into your life. You want Jesus on the throne of your life. You're willing to yield control of your life to Him. You don't want to live apart from Him any longer.

Pray the following prayer with me right now. (You can pray it even if you've already committed your life to Him.)

> *Dear God, I haven't been following You the way You want me to. I acknowledge that I've been running my own life. I'm sorry for all the times I messed up. Please forgive me all my sins. Please come into my life today. Please sit on the throne of my life. I want to trust You as my God. Thank You for loving me. I love You. I accept Your offer of eternal life.*

When you pray this prayer, you acknowledge that you've been living your life apart from God, and you ask God to forgive your sins. The moment you ask for forgiveness, God forgives you.

The next part of the prayer asks Jesus to come into your life and take control. He wants you to ask Him to do that every day. Are you uncomfortable with that part? Think of it this way: Corporations have financial and business managers. The owners hire people to control the company. Even some wealthy individuals hire financial planners. In this prayer you are asking Jesus to be your "life manager." Is He qualified? Absolutely! He loves you. He has no other agenda other than what is best for you. He is all-wise. He owns the universe. He is building a home in heaven for you (see John 14:2, 3). This is only the short version of His resume. Keep reading His letter to you—the Bible—to learn more about Him.

So, ask God to be your God, your Life Planner, your Life Manager, and your Friend. He's just waiting for you to ask. Maybe you've already reached the point where He is all those things for you. Just remember that you must request this every day. God won't force His love on you. He wants you to ask for it. This is spiritual health—a healthy relationship with God.

The blessing of belonging

At the beginning of the chapter, we stated that religion and spirituality are not synonymous, though they are both important to spiritual health. Spirituality has to do with our relationship with God. Religion has to do with a church: a group of people who believe in God and hold similar doctrinal views. The church is a vehicle through which you live out your spiritual experience with God and share your spiritual life with others. It's God's way of bringing His people together. Christians need worship time together. We need to pray, study, praise God, and worship together. Being part of a church provides a sense of belonging.

Participating actively in a church by worshipping regularly with fellow believers benefits you not only spiritually but also physically. A six-year research project involving 3,968 individuals ages 65 to 101 confirmed that. It showed that spirituality alone—believing in or having a personal experience with God—did not provide full health benefits. Those who attended religious services at least once a week had a 46 percent increase in life expectancy over the other study participants.[2]

Dr. Steen, who is eighty-four, is an example of someone who loves to be involved in church. He still teaches a Bible study group, even though he has a serious eye problem. He has a machine to magnify his Bible and other books so he can read. He refuses to let his vision impairment hinder his involvement. Church is important to him. It continues to give meaning to his life.

Bryce is ninety-eight—an age he considers very young. He has his personal time with God each morning after breakfast, and despite all the other activities he participates in, he finds time to act as a deacon in his church. He is excited about spending time with God and sharing with others the insights God has given him.

Bryce and Dr. Steen are not alone. Many others have discovered the incredible benefits of being part of the body of believers. They understand how important this connection is to their spiritual health. Not only is church involvement important for spiritual health, it also nurtures the other five areas of health because these areas are so intertwined. Let's see how religious and spiritual health relate to the other five.

1. Physical health. God wants you to enjoy good health. In Old Testament times, He told His people, "Worship the LORD your God, and his blessing will be on your food and water. I will take away sickness from among you. . . . I will give you a full life span"

(Exodus 23:25, 26). He still wants that for us today. He's ready to heal you physically and, most importantly, spiritually. Often these two go together—just look at the miracles Jesus performed in the New Testament.

The concept of prime-time living is based on biblical and scientific research that will show you how to reduce disease in your life. First, however, you must examine your spiritual health. You may have unresolved issues with God that are impeding your physical health. Spiritual health affects physical health.

2. Financial health. God promises that He'll prosper you when you follow biblical principles of financial management. The most important concept is to return to God a portion of the blessings He has given you. " 'Bring the whole tithe into the storehouse, that there may be food in my house. Test me in this,' says the LORD Almighty, 'and see if I will not throw open the floodgates of heaven and pour out so much blessing that you will not have room enough for it' " (Malachi 3:10). God owns everything. When you're faithful to Him, He'll take care of you.

3. Intellectual health. Both church attendance and Bible study provide mental stimulation. Listening to the pastor's sermons keeps your mind active. Making connections from auditory input challenges your thought process. Bible study strengthens the neural pathways in your brain. You've probably heard the saying "Use it or lose it." Bible study uses your brain power so that you won't lose it. The Bible vitalizes the mind as no other book can.

In that Friday evening worship service I mentioned in an earlier chapter, ninety-three-year-old Mary Ann was not only present but leading the music. She sees a threefold benefit from her involvement with church activities: social—meeting with neighbors and friends; intellectual—keeping her mind active by using her musical talents; and spiritual—developing a closer relationship with God.

4. Emotional health. Research shows that those who attend church are less likely to experience depression and anxiety. A three-stranded thread runs through the experience of people who attend church. They tend to experience love, forgiveness, and trust in God—all elements leading to peace of mind and a sense of security and belonging.

Love is the essence of who God is. It is also one of the greatest motivating factors for trying to become more emotionally healthy. Those who have loving relationships are more likely to work hard to maintain those relationships through emotional connection. Forgiveness—one of the fundamental teachings of most churches—is another important contributor to emotional health. It helps relieve anger, bitterness, and guilt. And trust in God leads to higher levels of happiness and joy. That's because those who trust God know that He will care for them, leaving them free from worry.

5. *Social health.* Those who are active in their church find friends there. Most churches provide numerous social opportunities, such as dinners, musical programs, picnics, and holiday programs. We'll discuss further the spiritual significance of friends in the chapter on social health, and we'll cite principles from the Bible about how to develop closer friendships.

Living the Christian life

An expert in the law asked Jesus, "What is the greatest commandment?"

Jesus replied, " ' "Love the Lord your God with all your heart and with all your soul and with all your mind." This is the first and greatest commandment. And the second is like it: "Love your neighbor as yourself" ' " (Matthew 22:37-39).

This was not an "either/or" answer. Jesus didn't say, "Some of you should focus on debating spiritual topics and forget all about your neighbor." Neither did He say, "If you are actively taking care of those in your community, you don't have to think about God." These two parts of spiritual health are like your two legs. Which leg is more important to you? Both legs are equally important, right? If you didn't have one of them, you'd find getting around to be difficult. Being a Christian also takes two legs: loving God and loving man. You can't stand on one leg for very long. You can't love God and be indifferent to others. Neither can you truly love people and be indifferent to God. True love comes only from God.

Living as a Christian means three things: making a commitment to follow God, continuing to develop a relationship with Him, and loving and caring for others. Being a Christian is like being married. First there is the wedding. In the wedding, both bride and groom make a commitment—their marriage vows. They promise to love, cherish, and honor each other. To be a Christian also means making a commitment. God wants you to ask Him to stay on the throne of your life. And just as the wedding is the ceremony that marks the commitment to marriage, so baptism is the ceremony marking people's commitment to becoming Christians.

After the wedding comes the marriage. It is the relationship— the life the bride and groom share. Having a happy marriage requires both the original commitment and a continuing relationship. To live as a Christian, you must live your life with God, continuing to develop a dynamic relationship with Him. God wants that kind of a relationship with you. Jesus says, "I am standing outside your house ringing the doorbell. If you want me to, I will come in and eat with you. I want to spend time with you" (my paraphrase of Revelation 3:20).

The third aspect of being a Christian is loving and caring for others. In marriage, that is a lifelong, joyful responsibility. In 1 Corinthians 13, Paul describes true love:

> Love is patient, love is kind. It does not envy, it does not boast, it is not proud. It is not rude, it is not self-seeking, it is not easily angered, it keeps no record of wrongs. Love does not delight in evil but rejoices with the truth. It always protects, always trusts, always hopes, always perseveres (verses 4-7).

This is the kind of love that, with God's help, Christians should exhibit to all those around them.

In some ways, spiritual health is like a journey. Some people travel all through life looking toward the next destination—high school, college, marriage, children, empty nest, retirement—and missing the significance of where they are right now. The same may be true in our spiritual experience. We may look to something far in the future and miss some of the wonderful blessings God is giving us right now. Sometimes the journey is just as important as the destination.

The spiritual journey is full of peaks and valleys. It's not always a walk in the park; sometimes it's more like climbing a series of mountains separated by lonely valleys. Walking up the mountain is difficult, but the view from the top makes it all worthwhile. For a while you're above the clouds, breathing in the fresh, cool mountain air. Then you descend again into the valley experiences of life. The sun is hot, and the refreshing mountain air is just a fleeting memory.

You'll face painful experiences and failures in life; you probably already have. When you go through those valleys, Jesus is just as available as He is during the mountaintop experiences. No matter where you are in the journey, you don't have to go through it alone. Jesus wants you to learn to lean on Him in the rough parts of the journey. If life had only mountaintop views, you couldn't benefit from the incredible lessons and blessings you can receive only through the difficult valley experiences.

The four P's of spiritual health

If spiritual life is like a journey, here is where the rubber meets the road. How can you have spiritual health? What does it look like? Examine the four P's of spiritual health: *perspective, purpose, priorities,* and *plan.*

Perspective. Every time I fly, I am amazed by how quickly everything on earth shrinks as the plane ascends toward the clouds. The perspective is so different. When you are spiritually healthy, your perspective differs. Things that may seem impossible when you are on your own seem easily accomplished when God is on your side. Not only can you look at the world from the perspective of a conqueror, but you also have the privilege of looking back at all the ways God has led you and blessed you in the past. Take the time to write out the story of your spiritual journey. Condense it to one or two pages so you can share it easily with others. (This would be a great activity for a small group or an "I Belong" group—see chapter 9 for more information.)

Purpose. I've heard older people ask, "Why am I still here? I'm not good for anything." That's not true! Having a spiritual life gives you purpose. You are God's special child. He created you to bless others with the love He's given you. You can always find ways to brighten someone else's day.

You can give the gift of encouragement even if you are confined to your bed. At the memorial service for an eighty-nine-year-old neighbor of ours, his caregiver tearfully shared what a ray of light he'd been to her. You may never know the results of your encouraging words. Just know that what you say can make a huge difference. Helping others will bring meaning into your life. That's a guarantee!

Here are some suggestions for living out your Christian love for others:

- Do prayer ministry (in person, by phone, or through the Internet).
- Volunteer as a parish nurse or assistant.
- Mentor younger Christians.
- Lead a Bible study group.
- Do hospitality ministry.
- Start an "I belong" group (see chapter 9).
- Get involved in your church's activities.
- Plant flowers in the church yard (with permission).
- Tell Bible stories to neighbor children.
- Help an older neighbor with a special need.
- Baby-sit for a single mom occasionally.
- Adopt a grandchild (a neighborhood or church child from a single-parent home).
- Give everyone you meet a big smile.

This list is meant just to get you started. God may have something completely different in mind for you. Ask Him.

Priorities. What is most important to you? Keeping your spiritual/religious value system in mind, write down what you consider important. Once you have your list, don't let the urgent events of life crowd out the people who are important to you—including God. Do first things first, then everything else afterward. The quality of your choices determines the quality of your life.

Plan. Now that you have established your priorities, create a plan of action. It may look something like this:

I will spend time with God every day by reading and reflecting prayerfully on His Word and keeping a prayer journal.

I will allow God to show me where He wants me to grow. I will glorify Him by allowing Him to sanctify me so that I can reflect His character.

I will learn more about God and become settled in His Word by studying and memorizing Bible passages. I will take a Bible class or join a Bible study group.

I will share the blessings God has given me by participating in a ministry or church activity as He directs.

These four P's are simply suggestions to jump-start your spiritual health. Be open to the prompting of the Holy Spirit as you prepare this list. Completing it may take several months of listening to God; you may even change some things you initially put on the list. Watch for God to reveal His will for you.

Spiritual maturity

Jesus had a disciple with an attitude. Because of his temper, he had the nickname Son of Thunder. John didn't remain that way though. He matured in his spiritual journey until eventually he became known as John the Beloved. Love permeates his writings. Jesus tells all of us to mature spiritually. "In a word, what I'm saying is, *Grow up.* You're kingdom subjects. Now live like it. Live out your God-created identity" (Matthew 5:48, *The Message*).

A friend of mine, eighty-four-year-old Glen, shows what it is like to be spiritually healthy. He was president of the British Columbia Conference of Seventh-day Adventists when he retired at age sixty-seven. Six weeks later, he was back to work on a stipend basis. He then retired a second time to do interim pastoral work for eighteen months at two different churches, later adding a third church. What keeps him going? His immediate reply is, "It is what the Lord has done." He adds, "Trust in God takes the stress out; life belongs to God."

Glen has retired again to do stewardship training seminars—"just one or two a month," he says. With a smile on his face, he gives God the credit. "Some of my richest spiritual experiences and sharing have come since my retirement. I have not peaked spiritually. I am still growing. . . . God is good."

HOMEWORK:

1. Write out the story of your personal spiritual journey. Include ways you feel God has directed your decisions and blessed you. Try to condense it down to a page so you can easily share it with others.
2. Which throne diagram fits your relationship with God right now?
3. John, one of the twelve disciples, had two nicknames—the one that people gave him was superseded by a better one after he met God personally. Do you have a nickname because of some negative character trait that you would like God to change for you? If so, ask Him right now to do that.

---

1. Carol A. Miller, *Nursing for Wellness in Older Adults: Theory and Practice,* fourth ed. (Philadelphia: Lippincott Williams Wilkins, 2003), 148.

2. Edward Schneider and Elizabeth Miles, *Ageless: Take Control of Your Age and Stay Youthful for Life* (Emmaus, Pennsylvania: Rodale Press, 2003), 192.

CHAPTER 4

Physical Health,

Part 1: Nutrition, Water, and Becoming Active

by Mary-Alice White, R.D.

Ann was one of those "super seniors"—a spunky little lady who used the treadmill next to me every morning at the fitness center. Not only did she exercise regularly, but she also made incredibly good food choices. She was an inspiration to those even twenty years her junior. One day when Ann came to a wellness class I was teaching, someone mentioned Twinkies. Ann asked, "What are Twinkies?" Sweet treats like Twinkies were not a part of her dietary lifestyle. The food that comprised her diet was nutritious, and she enjoyed what she ate. She didn't even want to try Twinkies. I feel certain her lifestyle of good nutrition choices and exercise contributed to the fact that while she was in her eighties, she was still free of disease and enjoying every minute of her life.

One of the components contributing to successful aging is the lowering of one's risk of disease. A recent review of litera-ture sponsored by The Center for Disease Control and Preven-tion found that heart disease, cancer, and cerebral vascular dis-ease were the leading causes of death during the year 2000. In that year, these three diseases contributed to more than 1.4 mil-lion deaths out of the total 2.4 million deaths in the United States. It is estimated that obesity due to poor diet and physical inactivity is second only to smoking as a cause of these diseases and death. Because poor diet and physical inactivity are such major hindrances to longevity, we will focus on these issues in this chapter and the next.

Restating the point, obesity is a serious problem. Like smoking, it's a major cause of death in our society. What can you do to avoid weight-related lifestyle diseases? Several things. And no matter how much effort it takes, doing so is worth it! By avoiding disease, you'll live a better quality, longer life, and you'll be able to enjoy prime-time aging.

If we look at what the majority of Americans eat and don't eat, we can learn better what we need to do to avoid disease. As a general rule, Americans

- eat too many refined and processed carbohydrates (such as white flour products) instead of eating an abundance of unrefined carbohydrates (such as whole grains).
- don't eat adequate amounts of fruits and vegetables.
- consume excessive amounts of unhealthy fats and don't eat enough healthy fats.
- eat more food than they actually need to maintain a desirable body weight.
- don't drink enough water.

These are five major problems to consider. Although nutrition includes other issues, if you correct these five, you'll dramatically change your health. Let's look at how they affect health and at how making changes in these areas will allow you to avoid disease.

Nutrition 101

Before we address the above issues, let's review some basic information about nutrition. There are six nutrient categories that your body needs to maintain health: carbohydrates, protein, fat, vitamins, minerals, and water. Each of these nutrients plays an important role in the normal functioning of your body. If you choose your foods and beverages wisely—eating a variety of foods that are in as natural a state as possible and drinking adequate amounts of water—you can obtain the nutrients necessary to keep your body healthy.

1. Carbohydrates

The first of the five problems involves a misunderstanding of carbohydrates. With the increased incidence of obesity and diabetes today, many people are trying to eliminate as many carbohydrates as possible from their diets. Food companies are catering to those who are attempting to lose weight by reducing their carbohydrate intake while eating unlimited amounts of protein.

However, carbohydrates have gotten a bad rap. Before we accuse all carbohydrates of making us fat, spiking our blood sugars, and contributing to insulin resistance, we need to take a closer look at this vitally important nutrient. Carbohydrates provide our bodies with glucose. One hundred percent of the carbohydrates we eat will be turned into glucose. Glucose is the ready fuel that the body burns for energy. It feeds the brain, which needs an ever-present supply of glucose to function properly. The body will store the glucose it doesn't need for immediate use as glycogen, a ready reserve for quick glucose needs. And, of course, beyond storing it as glycogen, the body can also convert the excesses to fat. This fat circulates in the bloodstream as triglycerides, and the body then stores it in all the places we would rather not have it stored!

It's because of this last point that many people have condemned all carbohydrates. But not all carbohydrates are created equal. They differ in their construction and in the reactions they cause. Carbohydrates are usually classified as either simple or complex. Simple carbohydrates are sugars. They are usually digested rapidly. Table sugar, honey, molasses, and the natural sugar in fruit are examples of simple sugar. In contrast, complex carbohydrates are starches consisting of long chains of glucose molecules that generally take longer for the body to process. Contained in this group of complex carbohydrates are starches such as pasta, rice, potatoes, corn, cereal, and others.

Unfortunately, carbohydrates are classified only as simple or complex, not according to how refined they are—a more important consideration. Food processors alter many carbohydrates, changing them greatly from their natural state. They're refined to such an extreme that they no longer retain their original, distinct characteristics, including how they behave in the body. However, if we classify carbohydrates on the basis of refined/processed and unrefined/unprocessed, we find that many *refined* complex carbohydrates will cause sudden rises in blood glucose levels. The *unrefined* carbohydrates, both simple and complex (the ones that come to us as God created them, unaltered by humans) still contain all the original nutrients and fiber. When carbohydrates are refined or processed, nutrients are lost in varying amounts. In addition, much of the all-important indigestible carbohydrate—fiber—is lost. The result is a food product that is not nutritionally up to par with its original counterpart. Lost or decreased nutrients impact our health, as does the loss of fiber.

Whole grains—complex, unrefined carbohydrates—are an excellent source of a large variety of nutrients and fiber. The fiber in whole, unrefined grains protects us against diabetes, heart disease, and gastrointestinal problems such as constipation and diverticulosis. The wide variety of nutrients in whole grains may also play a significant role in helping to reduce the risk of certain cancers. The majority of Americans eat less than one serving of whole grains per day, and they take in an average of only ten to twelve grams of fiber a day. The recommended amount is a minimum of twenty-five grams of fiber a day. That's a problem.

Evaluate your current eating habits. Are you drinking fruit juices to the exclusion of eating the whole fruit? How many foods in your pantry are refined carbohydrates or contain mostly refined carbohydrates? Do you read labels and lists of ingredients to determine if the food lists whole wheat?

Some of you are thinking, *I couldn't live without my white toast and cornflakes for breakfast. As for brown rice or whole-wheat pasta—I could never eat that whole grain stuff!* Let me give you some encouragement. You can educate your taste buds to enjoy foods that are more nutritious. Eventually, you'll stop craving the unhealthy foods you used to eat. Developing a taste for unfamiliar foods takes time. Start slowly, and begin to make some conscious decisions to eat the healthier, unrefined, unprocessed carbohydrates. To maximize the benefits of unrefined whole grains, try to eat several servings with each meal.

2. Fruits and vegetables

Fruits and vegetables contain many vitamins and minerals as well as the fiber and phytochemicals necessary for the normal functioning of your body. They are also low in calories. However, we don't eat enough of them! Current recommendations are that we eat five to nine servings a day. According to Behavioral Risk Factor Surveillance System (BRFSS) data, established by the Centers for Disease Control and Prevention, only 23 percent of the U.S. population consumes five or more servings of fruit and vegetables on a daily basis. The average daily intake of vegetables is only 3.1 servings—and that includes French fries and potato chips! Worse yet, the average daily intake of fruit is only 1.5 servings a day. And many of the fruits and vegetables we do eat are processed, resulting in decreased nutrients and fiber. A diet containing an abundance of colorful fruits and vegetables and low in unhealthy types of fat has been associated with reduced risk of heart disease, high blood pressure, stroke, cancer, and diabetes.

Data from the Nurses' Health Study have shown that those who consume eight or more servings of fruits and vegetables a day decrease their risk of stroke by 31 percent. The American Cancer Society's Cancer Prevention Study also showed some astounding results. Among the female subjects, those who consumed approximately five servings of fruits and vegetables a day had the least risk of dying during midlife (ages thirty-five to sixty-nine). Those women who ate much less than that had a 38 percent *increased* risk of dying early. The researchers found similar results among the men who participated in the study.

God has provided us with a rainbow of fruits and vegetables—green, yellow, orange, red, blue, purple, and white. Choosing a wide variety of colorful fruits and vegetables will help you get all the nutrients you need. And when you eat these foods as God created them, you will benefit from the full nutritional value that He has packaged into them. However, we consume too many foods that have been packaged in a less than desirable manner.

Take the potato for example—a staple vegetable in a typical American diet. Our love affair with the potato leads us to consume approximately 140 pounds per person per year. Unfortunately, we eat too many of them either as French fries or chips—both of which have been processed. In this refined and processed state, potatoes are not only devoid of many of their original nutrients but also cost much more. We complain when we have to pay eighty-nine cents a pound for beautiful Idaho baking potatoes. Yet we'll go to the snack aisle in the grocery store and think nothing of spending $2.19 for a 12-ounce bag of potato chips. That's $2.92 a pound for a spud that's been sliced and fried and now contains lots of fat and no significant nutrition!

The same is true for the apple. Taken whole, it is an excellent source of fiber and nutrients. However, when we make applesauce, apple juice, or apple pie, the processed apple provides fewer nutrients and less fiber. This processing of foods enables us to consume more calories, helping to contribute to the nationwide obesity problem. I'm not saying that you should never enjoy apple juice or applesauce. Though these foods are digested and metabolized rapidly, when consumed in moderation as part of a balanced diet, they can help you reach your health goals.

To add more vegetables to your diet, try

- a plate-size tossed salad as a meal, topped with garbanzo beans and roasted sunflower seeds and a healthy dressing (made with olive oil or tofu).
- legumes (dried beans) in the place of a high-fat meat.
- a glass of low-sodium vegetable juice with your meal.
- beverage mix of equal parts of pineapple juice and tomato juice—"pinato" juice. (It really does taste good!)
- ready-to-eat raw vegetables with lunch or as a snack, if you feel you must have a snack.

To include more fruit in your diet

- make a practice of eating at least one piece of fruit with each meal. This would be a healthier choice than eating the traditional high-calorie, sugary, fat-laden dessert.
- keep fresh fruit out on the counter in a bowl so it is readily available.

- incorporate fruit into salads—raisins and pineapple in carrot salads or raisins in a raw broccoli salad. Try tossing mandarin oranges into a fresh spinach salad, along with walnuts and sliced onions.
- add dried fruit to cooked or dry cereal.
- add fruit (banana, grape halves, raisins, etc.) to a sandwich made with natural peanut butter and whole-grain bread.
- take on the challenge of seeing how many new or unusual fruits and/or how many different colors of fruit you can eat in one day.

3. Fats

For more than thirty years, many people have tried to eliminate as much fat as possible from their diets. After all, professional diet gurus kept telling us we were eating too much fat. Unfortunately, in the process of reducing the total fat consumption from approximately 40 percent down to 34 percent, many people added more carbohydrates that are refined. During the years that followed, we have seen little change in the rate of heart disease. Instead, obesity and diabetes have increased. New research shows that we paid too much attention to total fat rather than to the type of fat consumed.

Like carbohydrates, fat comes in different types. And, as with carbohydrates, some types are healthy and some are unhealthy. The healthy fats are the polyunsaturated and monounsaturated types. These are the ones that are liquid at room temperature—the vegetable oils. Both polyunsaturated and monounsaturated fats lower the amount of bad cholesterol (LDL) in our blood and raise the amount of the good cholesterol (HDL).

The unhealthy fats are the saturated and trans fats—the ones that are solid at room temperature. Saturated fats raise the amount of bad cholesterol (LDL) in the blood. Trans fats *increase* the bad cholesterol, *decrease* the good cholesterol, and increase the triglyceride levels in the blood, which creates a variety of health problems. Unfortunately, Americans have been consuming too many unhealthy fats and not enough healthy fats.

Both saturated fats and trans fats are common on all the aisles in the grocery store. Saturated fats are found in both plant- and animal-based foods. The main problem is the large amount of saturated fat in animal foods and in processed foods. Too many people continue to eat red meat, whole milk, high-fat cheeses, ice cream, butter, and other foods high in saturated fat.

Food processors manufacture trans fats by hydrogenating liquid oil. Under pressure and in the presence of a catalyst, hydrogen is added to the oil. The end product is either solid or partially solid and more shelf stable. Food products containing the partially hydrogenated and hydrogenated fats do not spoil as rapidly because the fat doesn't go rancid as rapidly as liquid oil. While serving the food producers and grocery stores well, these fats have wreaked havoc on healthy hearts.

Trans fats are currently found in most margarines, vegetable shortening, deep-fried foods, commercially baked foods, and many ready-to-use baking mixes. Try to avoid these unhealthy fats by reading the list of ingredients and buying as little as possible of the products that contain partially hydrogenated oils. Fortunately, labeling laws now require companies to list with the other nutrition facts on the food label the amount of trans fat in the product.

Let's focus on the healthy fats: the mono- and polyunsaturated types. Plant foods usually contain all three types of fat (saturated, mono-, and polyunsaturated) in varying amounts. Among the foods that are largely monounsaturated are canola oil, olives and olive oil, peanut oil and peanuts, and most other nuts. The most common polyunsaturated oils are corn, soybean, and safflower oils, as well as the fat in fish.

The category of polyunsaturated fats contains several essential fatty acids that are necessary for good health because the body cannot make them. Common foods high in omega-3 fatty acids are canola (rapeseed) oil, flaxseed oil, flaxseed meal, English walnuts (with lesser amounts in black walnuts), wheat germ, soy and soy oils, deep green leafy vegetables, oils from fatty cold-water fish, and aquatic plants such as seaweed.

The bottom line is to choose healthy fats and avoid the unhealthy types—don't try to eliminate fat from your diet altogether. Here is a brief list of things you can do to achieve this goal:

- Avoid foods that are high in saturated fat, such as hamburgers, hot dogs, fried chicken, and high-fat dairy products such as cheeses, cream, butter, ice cream, and whole milk.
- Avoid trans fats. They're found in fast foods, baked items, baking mixes, many margarines, vegetable shortening, deep-fried foods, and many snack foods.
- Focus on eating the healthy fats, such as canola, soy, olive, flaxseed, and corn oils.
- Include a small handful of nuts in your diet daily.
- Eat foods in their natural state to get the good, natural fats your body needs; this includes nuts, olives, avocados, and even coconut in moderation. God doesn't make junk food!

A word about weight

The American Obesity Association says that obesity is a global epidemic. The National Health and Nutrition Examination Survey (NHANES) completed by the Centers for Disease Control and Prevention reports that 64.5 percent of adults living in the United States are overweight, nearly half of whom are obese. In the U.S., 127 million adults are overweight, 60 million are obese, and 9 million are severely obese.* Men between sixty-five and seventy-four years old and women between fifty-five and sixty-four years old have the highest prevalence of overweight and obesity. Some people decrease their activity level for one reason or another as they get older. If their eating habits remain the same, they gain weight.

Obesity is now the second leading cause of preventable death in the U.S. Approximately thirty medical conditions are associated with obesity, and current scientific research has established strong links between at least fifteen of these medical conditions and declining health and premature death. Among these conditions, according to NHANES III, are type II diabetes, coronary heart disease, high blood pressure, stroke, many types of cancers, and osteoarthritis.

---

*People with a body mass index (BMI) over 25 are generally considered *overweight*. The term *obese* is used to designate those who have a BMI over 30, and *severely obese* describes those with a BMI over 40.

How can you determine if you are overweight? Two of the most accurate approaches are a chart called the body mass index (BMI) and a test that measures waist girth. One can argue that getting on a regular bathroom scale is just as effective as using the BMI chart. However, the bathroom scale has a fatal flaw. Though it gives you an objective reading of your weight, it doesn't tell you what that weight is composed of—lean muscle or fat.

BMI is based on the relationship of your weight to your height. To determine your BMI, see the chart at the end of this chapter or follow this formula: Divide your weight in pounds by your height in inches. Divide the result by your height in inches again. Then multiply that number by 703. The result is your BMI.

What is a good BMI? Though scientists found that the risk of diabetes, heart disease, and hypertension begins to increase with BMIs of around 22, they have recommended levels between 18.5 and 25. If they made it any lower, the entire population would probably be considered overweight! If you have a BMI over 25, you would be considered overweight.

Another method of determining if your weight is a risk factor for disease is waist girth. Men with a waist girth measurement greater than thirty-nine inches are more than twice as likely as those with a smaller measurement to be at risk for cardiovascular disease. Women with a waist girth measurement greater than thirty-seven inches are more than three times more likely to be at risk for cardiovascular disease. To measure your waist girth, simply take a tape measure and measure the distance around your waist at the navel. The tape should be snug but not tight. And don't suck in your gut!

Using one of the above methods, what did you learn? Are you at risk for disease? If you are, don't be discouraged. Let's look at how you got that way and what to do about it. We'll look at three factors: lifestyle, what and how much you eat, and heredity.

Lifestyle. Your body is made up of lean body mass and fat. The lean body mass consists of muscle, bone, minerals, and other nonfat tissue. Muscle tissue is functional and active. It is like a car's engine. The bigger the engine, the more gas it will use, even when the engine is idling. Similarly, the more muscle tissue you have, the more calories you burn, whether exercising or resting. Large amounts of muscle tissue help you maintain a higher metabolism. When you become less active, you lose muscle tissue and your metabolism slows down. If you continue to consume the same amount of calories as you did when you were exercising, your body has no choice but to gradually gain weight. And guess what? It's not lean muscle tissue you gain—it's *fat,* that horrible excess stuff that accumulates in all the wrong places!

So, one obvious solution to the problem of weight gain is to get up and start moving. You burn more calories sitting than lying down. Likewise, you burn more calories standing than sitting. And, better yet, you burn more calories walking than standing still. So start moving! Participate in activities that will increase your percentage of muscle tissue—like resistance exercises, weight training on machines, lifting free weights—whatever you can do and will enjoy.

What you eat and how much you eat. The title of Bill Cosby's book *I Am What I Ate, and I'm Frightened* epitomizes what many people should be saying to themselves. Eating habits seem to be driven by food advertisements or by taste buds that demand to go to the closest fast-food establishment. Add to that the fact that America now has become a "grazing" society. Instead of sitting down to meals, many people eat at irregular intervals throughout the day. And as we have seen, many are not choosing healthy foods. Bad eating habits—excessive intake of refined sugars and other processed carbohydrates, unhealthy types of fats, and salt; and insufficient intake of fruits, vegetables, and fiber—have all contributed to the development of an overweight society susceptible to disease.

If we did the not-so-healthy things in moderation, they might not be so devastating. However, we do everything "bigger and better" today. For instance, my dinner plates are larger than the ones my grandmother owned. The silverware I bought recently to replace what we'd had for forty-four years is also larger—the new teaspoons are the size of the old soupspoons. Go into a restaurant, and you are served a meal on a plate that is the size of a serving platter. Supersize portions are readily available options to those who frequent fast-food establishments. Start today by analyzing what and how much you're eating. It isn't too late to change your eating lifestyle.

Heredity. We all would like to blame our extra weight on genes or a glandular problem. Maybe you wish your fat genes would shrink—just like the jeans in your closet seem to do. Our heredity *does* determine our body build and affects our propensity to accumulate fat in certain places. Studies of twins who were separated at birth and raised in different environments show they experienced similar patterns of weight gain. So heredity does indeed influence the way we are. But let's get real! How long are we going to blame someone else? How long are we going to persist in eating irresponsibly? How long are we going to refuse to take charge of our own health? Start now to become responsible for your own health.

What to do

This leads us to the next step. If you have excess fat, what can you do about it? Next to eating, dieting has become America's favorite pastime. Everyone is on a diet, and new diets pop up every week on TV and in magazines. If the old diets worked, why is there a proliferation of new ones? Most people think dieting is something temporary, only useful until they achieve a specific weight goal. But people have so little success in maintaining their weight loss because they haven't made permanent changes in their eating habits. To make weight loss permanent, I recommend the following lifestyle changes:

- Don't think diet. Think change in eating habits. Choose to eat healthy foods that will protect you against disease.
- Make changes slowly but deliberately. Don't try to change all your bad eating habits at once. And remember Mark Twain's words: "Old habits must be coaxed down the stairs one step at a time." Some people can make drastic changes overnight. But if you are like me, taking one step at a time is easier.
- Enlist the help of a supportive friend who won't become a "partner in food crimes" with you. Make yourself accountable to this friend.
- Record what and how much you eat and drink to help you

see the reality of what goes in your mouth. Seeing it stare back at you in black and white may make you aware of habits you didn't know you had.

- Learn what constitutes proper serving portions, and limit your portion size and number of servings.
- Set reasonable goals. Don't try to lose more than two pounds a week.
- Make exercise a regular part of your life.
- Join an exercise or weight-loss support group if this will assist you in achieving your goals.
- Focus on becoming more physically fit, not skinny! Remember, more muscle means you burn calories more efficiently. You may even gain a little weight when you begin exercising, because muscle weighs more than fat.
- View setbacks as losing small battles—not the whole war. The war isn't over.
- Enlist the help of the Lord.

Regarding that last point, for years I tried to eat right using my own willpower—without success. The cravings for flavors I had learned to enjoy in childhood didn't want to leave easily; my love affair with glazed donuts and Three Musketeers bars went with me into adulthood. Only after much prayer, reliance on the Lord's help, and a serious talk with my perverted taste buds did I find freedom from the tyranny of my bad habits.

The above suggestions are not exhaustive. There are many others. The most important thing is to admit what changes you need to make and then start to implement those changes gradually.

And be aware that people can go overboard. Some people think they must maintain the same figure they had in their twenties when they are in their eighties and nineties—a myth perpetuated by Hollywood. Even though their weight may be within normal limits, they think they need to lose five to ten pounds. Don't worry about a little extra padding. Being underweight may be just as dangerous to your health as is being overweight. I have seen older people hospitalized with a minor illness or minor surgery who had no fat reserves to draw from. The need for extra calories during an illness often goes unmet, especially by hospital food. As a result, the bodies of these people draw from the only remaining source of calories they have—muscle tissue. Those in this situation don't recuperate as well.

So, the bad news is that as a nation we are overweight. The good news is that we need *a little* stored fat to carry us through emergencies. Let's balance our "fat act" to remain healthy as we get older.

Wet your whistle

Water is not only the forgotten beverage but also the forgotten nutrient. Lack of water will kill a person more quickly than the absence of any other nutrient. Water accounts for approximately half of our total body weight. In addition to the water we drink, we get it from the other beverages we drink and the food we eat, and we also get it from metabolizing the food we eat.

We continually lose water from our bodies. We lose it through elimination (1-2.5 quarts per day), perspiration (12-14 ounces per day), and even through the air we exhale (a little more than a cup per day). Though we lose a lot of water via these routes, our bodies are master recycling plants. They reabsorb a large amount of water every day, depending on what they need. However, replacing the water we lose isn't all automatic. We need to help.

People's need for water varies with their weight and lifestyle. Generally, nutrition professionals recommend that adults drink approximately one quart of water for every thousand calories they consume, or one milliliter for every calorie consumed. That means if we eat two thousand calories a day, we need to drink about two quarts of water a day.

People depend on their thirst mechanism to remind them to drink water. However, as we age, our thirst mechanism may not work as well as it used to. That could put us at risk for dehydration. To emphasize our need for water, Tufts University personnel developed a Modified Food Pyramid for adults over seventy.[1] They recommend eight 8-ounce glasses of fluid a day. This is commonly recommended as an appropriate amount of fluid intake for those of all ages, but it does not appear on the regular food pyramid. The researchers at Tufts University put it in theirs to show how incredibly important water is to good health.

Nature's most wonderful fluid is water—pure water. Nothing can quench your thirst better. Nothing can cleanse your system better. Nothing can wet your whistle better.

Don't be satisfied with the status quo—poor dietary habits that lead to lifestyle diseases. Choose instead to eat more fruits and vegetables; more whole, unrefined grains; fewer refined and processed carbohydrates; and healthy fats in moderation. In addition to these positive eating changes, add physical activity and a serious commitment to maintain a healthy weight.

It's high time to honor the Creator by eating more healthfully and engaging in regular exercise and activity. When more people begin to do this, we will begin to see a decline in the diseases that are robbing people of good health. Avoiding disease is one of the ways you can enjoy prime-time aging now and in the future. You owe it to yourself to make that choice right now!

HOMEWORK

1. Write down some of the dietary changes you want to make.
2. If you haven't already done so, figure out your BMI. To determine your BMI, see the chart on the following pages or follow this formula: Divide your weight in pounds by your height in inches. Divide the result by your height in inches again. Then multiply that number by 703. For example, if you weigh 180 pounds and you are 5 feet 10 inches (70 inches) tall, the process would look like this:

   $180 \div 70 = 2.57$

   $2.57 \div 70 = .0367$

   $.0367 \times 703 = 25.8$

   A good BMI is between 18.5 and 25. A BMI over 25 is considered overweight, so at 25.8, the person in our example is slightly overweight.
3. List the things you do to stay active. What are some other things you could add to your schedule to work in more exercise?

---

1. <http://nutrition.tufts.edu/consumer/pyramid.html>.

Body Mass Index Chart

BMI	19	20	21	22	23	24	25	26	27	28	29	30	31	32	33	34	35	36
58	91	96	100	105	110	115	119	124	129	134	138	143	148	153	158	162	167	172
59	94	99	104	109	114	119	124	128	133	138	143	148	153	158	163	168	173	178
60	97	102	107	112	118	123	128	133	138	143	148	153	158	163	168	174	179	184
61	100	106	111	116	122	127	132	137	143	148	153	158	164	169	174	180	185	190
62	104	109	115	120	126	131	136	142	147	153	158	164	169	175	180	186	191	196
63	107	113	118	124	130	135	141	146	152	158	163	169	174	180	186	191	197	203
64	110	116	122	128	134	140	145	151	157	163	169	174	180	186	192	197	204	209
65	114	120	126	132	138	144	150	156	162	168	174	180	186	192	198	204	210	216
66	118	124	130	136	142	148	155	161	167	173	179	186	192	198	204	210	216	223
67	121	127	134	140	146	153	159	166	172	178	185	191	198	204	211	217	223	230
68	125	131	138	144	151	158	164	171	177	184	190	197	203	210	216	223	230	236
69	128	135	142	149	155	162	169	176	182	189	196	203	209	216	223	230	236	243
70	132	139	146	153	160	167	174	181	188	195	202	209	216	222	229	236	243	250
71	136	143	150	157	165	172	179	186	193	200	208	215	222	229	236	243	250	257
72	140	147	154	162	169	177	184	191	199	206	213	221	228	235	242	250	258	265
73	144	151	159	166	174	182	189	197	204	212	219	227	235	242	250	257	265	272
74	148	155	163	171	179	186	194	202	210	218	225	233	241	249	256	264	272	280
75	152	160	168	176	184	192	200	208	216	224	232	240	248	256	264	272	279	287
76	156	164	172	180	189	197	205	213	221	230	238	246	254	263	271	279	287	295

Body Mass Index Chart (continued)

BMI	37	38	39	40	41	42	43	44	45	46	47	48	49	50	51	52	53	54
58	177	181	186	191	196	201	205	210	215	220	224	229	234	239	244	248	253	258
59	183	188	193	198	203	208	212	217	222	227	232	237	242	247	252	257	262	267
60	189	194	199	204	209	215	220	225	230	235	240	245	250	255	261	266	271	276
61	195	201	206	211	217	222	227	232	238	243	248	254	259	264	269	275	280	285
62	202	207	213	218	224	229	235	240	246	251	256	262	267	273	278	284	289	295
63	208	214	220	225	231	237	242	248	254	259	265	270	276	282	287	293	299	304
64	215	221	227	232	238	244	250	256	262	267	273	279	285	291	296	302	308	314
65	222	228	234	240	246	252	258	264	270	276	282	288	294	300	306	312	318	324
66	229	235	241	247	253	260	266	272	278	284	291	297	303	309	315	322	328	334
67	236	242	249	255	261	268	274	280	287	293	299	306	312	319	325	331	338	344
68	243	249	256	262	269	276	282	289	295	302	308	315	322	328	335	341	348	354
69	250	257	263	270	277	284	291	297	304	311	318	324	331	338	345	351	358	365
70	257	264	271	278	285	292	299	306	313	320	327	334	341	348	355	362	369	376
71	265	272	279	286	293	301	308	315	322	329	338	343	351	358	365	372	379	386
72	272	279	287	294	302	309	316	324	331	338	346	353	361	368	375	383	390	397
73	280	288	295	302	310	318	325	333	340	348	355	363	371	378	386	393	401	408
74	287	295	303	311	319	326	334	342	350	358	365	373	381	389	396	404	412	420
75	295	303	311	319	327	335	343	351	359	367	375	383	391	399	407	415	423	431
76	304	312	320	328	336	344	353	361	369	377	385	394	402	410	418	426	435	443

Find your height in inches in the left-hand column. Look for the figure closest to your weight in the row to the right. The number at the top of the column is your Body Mass Index number (BMI).

CHAPTER **5**

Physical Health,

Part 2: The Importance of Exercise

In her working days, Charlotte Hamblin was an assistant nursing professor at Andrews University. Now retired, she is a very young eighty-five-year-old. She's getting ready to bicycle from one end of New Zealand to the other, a three-week trip. This trip will be similar to others she has taken. She will ride between seventy and eighty miles a day, stopping along the way to publicize the benefits of healthful living.

In 1993, Charlotte completed a big ride. Beginning in Vancouver, B.C., she biked up the Canadian Rockies and then all the way across Canada, ending in St. Johns, Newfoundland. She completed the trip in three months. This trip across Canada was her favorite. She especially enjoyed the beauty of the Rockies and the animals she saw along the way.

Charlotte has ridden her bike a total of fourteen thousand miles in all parts of the world. One of her scariest adventures occurred while she was bicycling in Nepal. Two robbers jumped out of an alley and started to chase her. She increased her speed, her heart pounding from the adrenalin. Eventually the sound of footsteps behind her faded away, but she kept pedaling hard for a long time just to be safe. That's just one of many stories Charlotte has to tell about her adventures and misadventures. She thinks the danger is worth it. She claims as her motto, "Life is what you put into it."

Today, at eighty-five, Charlotte takes no medications. Her daily routine includes riding her bicycle five miles before breakfast. Bicycling isn't the only thing she likes to do. She also loves hiking. Recent treks have taken her to the tops of Mount Adams in Washington State and Mount Hood in Oregon. She says, "Age has nothing to do with my activities." She's reaping the benefits of an active, healthy lifestyle.

You may say, "All that exercise is fine for Charlotte, but I can't do it!" It is true that not everyone can be a Charlotte Hamblin. However, you probably have at least one thing in common with Charlotte—you want to stay as young and healthy as possible. What is the single most effective thing you can do to stay healthy? The answer is simple: stay active physically. In a study about healthy aging conducted by the Centers for Disease Control, the researchers noted, "Nowhere is the gap wider between what we know and what we do than in the area of physical activity, and nowhere is the potential pay-off greater."[1] They concluded, "Although the risk of disease and disability clearly increases with advancing age, poor health is not an inevitable consequence of aging."[2]

So, the bad news is that the risk of disease and disability does increase as you get older. The good news is that aging doesn't mean poor health is inevitable. You can be healthy and energetic into your eighties and nineties. Research shows that lifestyle is more important than your genetic code in avoiding decline and deterioration of body and mind. In this chapter you will see how the lack of physical activity contributes to the downward spiral called normal aging and how regular physical activity is a significant component of prime-time living and prime-time aging.

The benefits of exercise

Here's a partial list of the benefits of regular exercise. It

- increases longevity.
- reduces functional dependence on others.
- reduces the risk of falls, fractures, and injuries by improving balance and coordination.
- reduces frailty and physical impairment.

- boosts the immune system, helping the body fight off infections.
- slows the biological aging process.
- improves enjoyment of life.
- maintains muscle mass and strength.
- reduces the risk of contracting the following diseases and disease conditions: heart and coronary artery disease; type II diabetes; colon and breast cancer; high blood pressure; obesity; osteoporosis; depression; stroke; peripheral vascular disease; and constipation.[3]

We find the best route to a healthy old age not by trying to cure any of the above diseases but by preventing them.

Because exercise provides so many benefits, we might think people would comply 100 percent to the recommendation to exercise daily. The reality is, however, that only 16 percent of adult Americans engage in vigorous exercise three or more times a week, and 23 percent engage in light to moderate sustained physical activity five or more days a week. That's a total of 39 percent. On the other end of the scale, 23 percent live a totally sedentary lifestyle, doing no exercise. That means the other 38 percent do some exercise but not regularly. This isn't very encouraging—and the situation is even worse among certain groups, including the elderly, women, minorities, and those with low income and education levels. Among those sixty-five and older, 43 percent are sedentary. Among those between the ages of sixty-five and seventy-four, only 6 percent engage in resistance or strength training.

As the Center for Disease Control (CDC) said, the gap between what we know about exercising and what we do is tremendous. The Department of Health and Human Services has begun a program called "Healthy People 2010." The goal is to increase the number of those who engage in light to moderate exercise thirty minutes a day, five days a week, from 23 percent to 30 percent and to increase the number of those engaging in vigorous exercise from 16 percent to 25 percent. That would still mean only 55 percent of Americans were getting regular exercise.

Disability

Everyone wants to enjoy a long, healthy life. People hope to remain mentally alert, mobile, and free of disability, and finally, to die without pain and suffering. Often, the aged worry more about being disabled than about dying. That's a valid concern. It is estimated that 37 percent of men and 55 percent of women eighty-five years of age and older depend on another person's help to perform daily activities. Researchers studied a group of 1,097 men and women ages sixty-five and up. They tracked them for ten years to determine the likelihood of men living to age eighty without disability and of women living to age eighty-five without disability. The results showed that 26 percent of men and 18 percent of women reached these ages without disability. The women were found to live longer but to have a greater rate of disability.[4]

Disability is determined by the person's ability to perform "activities of daily living" (ADLs). These ADLs include bathing, dressing, mouth care, hair care, mobility, food preparation, eating without assistance, bladder and bowel elimination, housekeeping, laundry, and money management. Obviously, the greater the level of disability, the more of these functions a person cannot perform.

Not every eighty-five- or ninety-year-old lives with disability. Many are disability free. Who are those at greater risk of becoming disabled or partially disabled?

One factor contributing to disability is the presence of a chronic disease, such as osteoarthritis, osteoporosis, hypertension, diabetes, depression or an anxiety disorder, lung disease, cardiovascular disease, or stroke. People with any of these chronic diseases are more likely to become disabled prior to death.

Another risk factor is obesity. Those who have a body mass index greater than twenty-seven have a 37 percent greater risk of some level of disability prior to death. A factor that goes hand-in-hand with obesity is the risk of living a sedentary lifestyle.

Falls and the injuries resulting from falls are two of the most serious risk factors that lead to disability. Every year about 30 percent of people in the older adult population fall. Half of those have fallen more than once. About 10 to 15 percent of the falls cause serious injury, such as a broken hip. Those who fall often face a decline in their ability to perform ADLs. Some will be confined to a nursing home. (Addendum A tells what you can do to reduce the risk of falls.)

Other risk factors contributing to disability are age, gender, and ethnicity. Whites generally suffer more disabilities than do those from other races.[5] And, as we've noted, females are more prone to disability—probably because as they age, they generally exercise less than do males, and thus, having less muscle mass, are more likely to become frail.

These latter risk factors are largely out of our control (except that women can choose to exercise more as they age). However, the others listed above are, at least to some extent, within our control. We *can* reduce our risk of disability.

Reducing disability

There are many reasons to include exercise as part of our life as we age. One of the most important reasons is to reduce the risk of disability. However, many have not taken the time to exercise. Maybe you feel it isn't as important for older people. Actually the reverse is true. The older you become, the more important exercise, particularly strength training, becomes. Unfortunately, only 6 percent of sixty-five- to seventy-four-year-olds do regular strength training. This figure drops to 4 percent above the age of seventy-five. Those in this age group face the greatest risk of disability.

Normal aging creates a vicious cycle. Many diminish their physical activity. This leads to reduced muscle strength, which in turn causes greater demand on muscles that are now smaller in mass. The stress on these muscles makes people tire more quickly. As a result, they do even less physical activity. This process has nothing to do with age and everything to do with activity level. Research shows that muscle strength need not decline to a level that affects daily life. It is extremely important that you maintain your reserves in both strength and aerobic capacity .

The *Merck Manual of Health and Aging* says:

> Exercise may be the closest thing to the fountain of youth available. It improves overall health and appearance. It can

maintain some of the body's functions that decline with aging. It can even restore some functions that have already declined. In addition, people who exercise—regardless of how much they weigh, whether they smoke, or whether they have a disorder—tend to live longer than those who do not exercise.[6]

Maintaining physical fitness pays wonderful dividends. The benefits of staying active begin the day you start exercising. You will begin to have more energy. You will not tire as easily. You will feel better about yourself. Your sleeping patterns will improve.

You may be saying to yourself, "This is all good, but I'm too out of shape." You may be out of shape (like well over half of the American population—especially those over fifty-five), but there is a solution. You can catch up!

Catching up means making up for something you should have already developed or accomplished. When students go to college and are not at an acceptable level scholastically in a particular subject, they are usually required to take a remedial course to attain a level of achievement they should have already attained. The remedial class is helping them catch up. Students don't walk away from college just because they need an extra class to help them achieve their goal. Catching up isn't bad or unusual. Everyone has different areas of strengths and weaknesses. Begin where you are, and take one step at a time.

How should you exercise? The answer depends on your physical condition, the level of conditioning you want to reach, and the type of exercise you enjoy or find convenient. FIT is an acronym that helps answer that question. "F" stands for frequency. How often should you exercise? The recommendation for aerobic exercise is five to seven times a week. For strength (weight, resistance) training, the recommendation is two to three times a week.[7] However, you can choose to do strength training every day and work upper body and lower body muscle groups on alternating days.

The letter "I" stands for intensity. Intensity involves the speed or difficulty at which you are exercising. Intensity can usually be classified as light, moderate, or vigorous. Most health benefits occur within the moderate range. Older adults should not attempt a vigorous intensity unless they're already in excellent condition. It is very important that you consult your physician before beginning an exercise regimen, especially if you are over fifty-five. Those who are not accustomed to exercise should begin slowly. Starting too vigorously may result in aches and pains. Start slowly and increase the intensity until you reach a level you feel comfortable with.

The letter "T" is for time. Decide how much time you can exercise. If you are just beginning, you may want to start with walking for five minutes. Others may start at ten or fifteen minutes. Whatever time frame you begin with, build up slowly to the recommended thirty minutes a day, most days of the week. Some researchers are even recommending up to sixty minutes a day, depending on one's ability level. If you choose thirty minutes a day, you may want to divide your time into three ten-minute segments throughout the day or fifteen minutes twice a day.

To enjoy the benefits of good physical health and to reduce the risk of disease and disability, you need four types of fitness training. These areas of fitness are aerobic (endurance), strength training (resistance), balance, and stretching. It is not necessary to engage in each one every day, but you should do each regularly. Let's look briefly at each area.

1. Aerobic exercise

This is the first type of exercise we usually think of when the subject of exercise arises. Aerobic exercise requires the body to use oxygen from the air in order to produce the energy necessary for the muscles to work. The health benefits include a strengthening of the heart and lungs, burning calories, and increasing your endurance.

Some examples of aerobic exercise are walking, running, biking, rowing, swimming, skating, and mowing the yard using a push mower. Aerobic exercise falls into two categories: weight bearing and nonweight bearing. Weight-bearing aerobic exercise, like walking and running, gives the added benefit of strengthening the bones, providing protection against osteoporosis. Swimming, biking, and rowing are nonweight-bearing aerobic exercises. They're excellent forms of aerobic exercise for those who need to avoid impact. Those with joint problems or those who are overweight may want to consider nonweight-bearing exercises in moderation.

Aerobic exercise helps reduce disability in several ways. First, and most importantly, it helps prevent disease, including the number-one killers in the U.S.: cardiovascular disease, stroke, and diabetes. These diseases are most likely to result in disabilities. Second, aerobic exercise helps reduce the negative impact of existing disease. Exercise is therapeutic and can be part of the disease treatment process. Third, aerobic exercise can reduce the risk of obesity that may contribute to the above named diseases.

Regular aerobic exercise is directly related to lower mortality rates. The Good Health Practice Study on sixteen thousand Harvard alumni showed physical activity was the best predictor of longevity. The least active men had a mortality rate two times higher than the most active men. The results among the women were even more astounding. Women who exercised the least were three times more likely to die compared to the women who engaged in the most exercise.[8]

2. Strength training/resistance exercise

This type of exercise involves the contraction of muscles against some form of resistance. Many overlook strength training. As we saw earlier, only 16 percent of the population does it on a regular basis—and only 6 percent in the sixty-five to seventy-four age category. However, it's in the later years of life that maintaining strength becomes particularly important. Prime-time aging means staying strong and maintaining a high energy level so you have the vitality to accomplish all your goals.

You may choose to lift weights, do push-ups and sit-ups, pull on a large piece of elastic band, or use machines at your local gym. You need not feel intimidated there. I recall saying to one of the young guys in the gym where I exercise, "You young guys must really laugh at us older guys." He replied, "Laugh—no way! We respect you and look up to you."

The area of strength training is where many need to do the most catching up. If you fail to do so, you may eventually find that performing simple tasks such as carrying in the groceries or opening a can of food is very tiring or even impossible. If this occurs, you will become dependent on someone else to care for you. So, while keeping the heart muscle strong is essential, keeping the arm and leg muscles strong is important too.

> Clinical experience and limited studies suggest that people who maintain or improve their strength and flexibility may be better able to perform daily activities, may be less likely to develop back pain and may be better able to avoid disability, especially as they advance into older age. Regular physical activity also may contribute to better balance, coordination, and agility, which in turn may help [them] prevent falls.[9]

By the time you reach retirement age, you have lost muscle strength and have less muscle mass. "Between the ages of thirty and eighty, mean strength of back, arm, and leg muscles drops as much as 60 percent, largely reflecting a progressive loss of muscle mass at an average rate of 4 percent per decade from twenty-five to fifty and 10 percent per decade thereafter."[10]

Whether you choose to join a gym or do some strength training in your home, start only with what you feel comfortable doing. You don't have to lift heavy weights to maintain or build more muscle; you just need to do some form of strength training regularly.

3. Balance

A third element of exercise is balance. Good balance helps prevent falls. Poor balance tends to create a sense of fear and lowers your willingness to continue a particular activity. Here are some simple balance activities that you can do at home:

- Practice tandem walking—that is, walking heel to toe. You may want to practice it between chairs so you don't risk a fall.
- Stand on one leg for fifteen to twenty seconds, then on the other leg. Advanced: stand on one leg and attempt to raise the other leg. You may even be able to put a sock on or tie your shoes while balancing yourself.
- Close your eyes while standing on one leg. Advanced: tandem walk with your eyes closed. Be very careful not to fall. Do this exercise *only* if you have good balance.
- Ride a bicycle. (Always wear a helmet.)
- Use a mini trampoline.

4. Stretching

This helps lengthen muscles and tendons, improving flexibility—which helps prevent injury. Stretching also helps maintain range of motion, something that's particularly important as you age. You "should stretch only after warming up or exercising, when the muscles are warm and less likely to tear."[11] And to avoid injury, you should not bounce in an attempt to stretch your muscles.

Beginning your fitness program

To begin your fitness program:
- Consult your physician to make sure you have no precluding health conditions.
- Start slowly. You will enjoy exercising more if your muscles aren't yelling at you. Muscles will respond to a gradual increase of intensity and duration. Find a comfortable level and begin. Aging muscles are more easily injured and take more time to heal, so don't overdo it!
- Develop a positive attitude toward exercise.
- Find the exercises that you enjoy. If you enjoy what you're doing, you're more likely to continue.
- Put some variety into your exercise program—several different exercises that you enjoy.
- Make exercise socially enjoyable. Find an exercise buddy— perhaps even two or three. Golfers always have partners. However, you may be one of those who prefer to use their exercise

time to "prayer walk." Some people like to pray for all the occupants of the homes they walk past.

- Set goals—short-term, midrange, and long-term goals with specific things you want to accomplish and the date by which you want to accomplish them. Be realistic.
- Reward yourself when you achieve your goals.

Don't gear down physically for retirement. If you gear down, you'll spiral down. This can occur quickly. You might begin by giving up just a few daily activities, cutting back a little on your workload. However, then your muscles begin to deteriorate, and you may start to notice it takes a little more effort to open that can or carry that heavy box. It isn't too late. You have a choice. Don't gear down. Gear up. Be active.

HOMEWORK

1. Evaluate your level of fitness. How often do you exercise? Are you meeting the recommended levels?
2. Talk to your doctor about developing a fitness plan or stepping up the one you already have. Set goals and dates to reach those goals.
3. Start exercising! (For some suggestions, see addendum B, which begins on page 74.)

---

1. *Healthy Aging: Preventing Disease and Improving Quality of Living Among Older Americans 2001,* Department of Health and Human Services, Centers for Disease Control and Prevention.

2. Ibid.

3. Maria A. Fiatarone Singh, "Exercise to Prevent and Treat Functional Disability," *Clinical Geriatric Medicine* 18 (2002), 431–462.

4. Leveille, Guralnik, *American Journal of Epidemiology* 149, no. 7.

5. Ibid.

6. Mark H. Beers, ed., *The Merck Manual of Health and Aging 2004* (Whitehouse Station, N.J.: Merck Research Laboratories, 2004), 806.

7. Ibid.

8. Berkman and Syme, *Journal of Epidemiology* 109, no. 2, 186.

9. Russell R. Pate, et al, "Physical Activity and Public Health," *Journal of the American Medical Association* 273, no. 5 (Feb. 1, 1995): 404.

10. Joseph A. Buckwalter, "Decreased Mobility in the Elderly: The Exercise Antidote," *The Physician and Sports Medicine* 25, no. 9 (1997).

11. *Merck Manual,* 810.

Addendum A: Reduce Your Risk of Falling

You can do a number of things to reduce your risk of falling. First, make sure your house is adequately lit with either natural or electric light. Don't try to save on the electric bill by not turning on the lights.

Second, watch how you walk. Be careful on stairs. The first and last steps seem to cause the most falls on stairs. You should also watch for uneven surfaces, such as curbs, broken sidewalks, and especially throw rugs. Regarding the latter, perhaps you should do as the name implies—throw them out. Similarly, avoid littering the traffic pattern of your house even temporarily with chairs, boxes, or electric cords.

Third, maintain both your sense of balance and your muscles— particularly those in your legs. You can accomplish this through a program that includes both strength and stretching exercises plus exercises for your sense of balance. (For suggestions regarding these exercises, see the addendum that follows.)

Addendum B: Exercise Activities That People Enjoy

You don't have to go to a gym and get on the treadmill to get valuable exercise. I interviewed several older adults about things they love to do that give them the exercise they need.

1. Gardening

"Gardening—that's where you get a lot of exercise. . . . That's why I do it," says Herman Messer. He's eighty-five and has a large, beautiful garden every year. He lives in an independent retirement community that provides garden spots for the residents. Herman says he gets cardiovascular exercise when he hoes.

Geri Duckett, seventy-nine, has both flower and vegetable gardens. Her reason? "I love to see things grow, kind of like watching children grow," she says. For Geri there are also spiritual blessings. "It's like partnering with God. He provides the life, the sunshine, and the rain. I do the planting and nurturing. I also get in some hard work, but it is so satisfying."

My own mother, Dolly Reay, gardens to keep two freezers full of fruit and vegetables. "I do it for exercise also," she says. The garden keeps her going in the spring and summer and into early fall. She has the added benefit of enjoying a feast of healthy foods all year.

Gardening is a great way to obtain enjoyable, rewarding exercise. It helps to maintain strong muscles, heart, and lungs. In addition, gardeners benefit from being in the sunshine and fresh air.

2. Water exercises

Swimming is an enjoyable way to get your exercise if you love water. You can increase your heart rate as high as you need to and burn a lot of calories in the process. For those whose exercise options are limited because of arthritis or other painful chronic diseases, swimming is an excellent alternative to weight-bearing exercise.

Carol does water aerobics for one hour four to five days a week. She says, "The greatest benefit is I don't have any pain after my water aerobics." When she tries other forms of exercise, her hips and lower back hurt. She's been exercising this way for ten years now. She says she could always find a reason not to walk, "but the pool—I meet my seven friends there." Carol says she gets an excellent cardiovascular workout along with strength training and also a stretching workout during the same session.

3. Walking

Walking is the exercise of choice for many older persons. Suzanne Leveille found, in her research with older adults, that 58 percent of her study participants walked for their primary exercise.

Margie Gray, eighty-two, has walked every day for twenty-five years. She walks an hour and a half every morning, and then in the afternoon she walks her dog, Bo, half a mile. "I like the walk, and he likes it too," she says. When Margie lost her husband four years ago, the physician who had cared for her husband remarked, "Getting your dog was the best thing you could have done for yourself."

Bob, another fan of walking, recently suffered a stroke. As a result, he was left with weakness on one side of his body and a slight limp. He walks every day with his wife at his side to help him. Walking has helped him in his recovery.

4. Golf

Golf, a sport that involves a lot of walking, is an enjoyable way to spend a morning with your spouse or friends. Golf is low-intensity exercise, but by the time you complete the round, you feel you've had a workout.

Jack Duckett, eighty-seven, plays golf with his friends once a week. Jack plays for relaxation and fellowship. He says, "The score doesn't matter. A physician friend who is involved in health promotion told me, 'I don't know if golf helps you live longer, but the fresh air and sunshine are good for you.'" In addition to the fresh air, sunshine, and exercise, Jack is enhancing his social health.

5. Bicycling

Bicycling can be an indoor or outdoor sport. Indoor biking is great for FIT (frequency, intensity, time). You can bike every day—rain or shine, hot or cold. You can ride while catching up on the daily news or watching your favorite game show or video. You can easily control the intensity level—light, moderate, or intense. And you can choose how long you want to ride. Outdoor biking has the advantage of changing scenery, fresh air, sunshine, and sharing the path with a bicycling friend. Al Hess, seventy-four, bicycles thirty to forty minutes a day, five days a week. His arthritis doesn't stop him from riding hills and completing his course on a nearby track. He covers five to six miles a day.

Brent turned sixty in May of 2004. He's been biking for twelve years now. He just recently got back from a three-week bike tour of France. During the spring, summer, and fall, he typically rides sixty to one hundred miles per week. He says he's in better shape now than he was in his twenties.

6. Hiking

Hiking can take you through beautiful terrain. You can enjoy the pleasures of wildflowers, singing birds, wild animals, and the occasional rippling stream. The exercise can be vigorous, moderate, or light, depending on the incline and your speed. Hiking is great for burning calories.

The Halls—Don, fifty-seven, and particularly Phyllis, fifty-eight, are avid hikers. Phyllis has a goal of hiking the Pacific Coast Rim Trail. She and Don have been hiking together all their married life. "It is something we both enjoy and can do together. . . . It gives us a lifetime of memories." Hiking gives them a chance to do something active with their friends and allows Don to take photographs along the way, one of his hobbies.

7. Running/jogging

Jogging is a good way to obtain a vigorous workout in a short period of time and burn a lot of calories—especially a jog that lasts thirty to sixty minutes. Jogging also increases lung capacity. Joggers usually work out at a high level of intensity and enjoy it. Some even aspire to run marathons.

This list is in no way exhaustive. There are many other forms of aerobic exercise, such as rowing, racquetball, tennis, and basketball. It doesn't matter what you do. Choose something you enjoy and just do it!

CHAPTER 6

Financial Health:

Planning for Your Financial Future

by Gordon Botting, Dr.P.H., C.H.E.S., Certified Financial Counselor

Retirement is a relatively new phenomenon made possible by the longevity of people today. At the turn of the past century, the average person lived to age forty-seven, as compared to the average person today who lives well into his or her seventies or eighties. Over the past thirty years, the growing numbers of those who live longer have become even more noteworthy. In 1960, Social Security cut two thousand checks for Americans one hundred years old. It is estimated that by the year 2010, it will be sending out one hundred thousand monthly checks to centenarians! Much of this increase in longevity is due to modern medical technology—drugs and vaccines have wiped out former killer diseases such as measles and small pox. But it is also due in part to the preventive lifestyle that has become part of our culture.

Because of this new era of long life, those looking forward to retirement must ask some important questions: How much money will we need to live after retirement? How will we foot the bills? Do we have enough? And is this just enough to survive, or will we live comfortably through our sunset years?

If you're fortunate enough to have planned for your retirement, you can now concentrate your energies on where you're going to retire and what sort of lifestyle you and your spouse will be able to enjoy. Unfortunately, a majority of individuals and married couples, particularly among the Baby Boomer generation—those born between 1946 and 1964—have not planned sufficiently. To have any sort of decent retirement, they'll have to take the above questions seriously.

Before you start calculating how much you will need financially for your retirement years, you need to ask this important question: "Do I really want to retire? And if not now, when?" If you answered the first question with a resounding, "Yes. I want to retire right now!" you need to ask yourself some more challenging questions. Remember, if you retire at fifty-five and live to the ripe old age of ninety-five, you'll have spent as much time in retirement as you have in the working period of your life. If you wait until you're sixty to retire, you will still spend more than one-third of your life in the "golden years." You may enjoy your job. Do you really want to leave? When you no longer have to go to work, how will you fill your days?

One of the most difficult social aspects of retirement is that your personhood is no longer defined by your career. The current generation of Baby Boomers is a group of guinea pigs. Through their experiences, they'll answer the question as to whether it's better to live longer and retire younger rather than to experience retirement as a brief period at the end of life, as earlier generations have. If your whole life has been wrapped up in your job, retirement can change your sense of belonging and self-worth. As one person described it, "When I announced I was going to retire, I became invisible." People treated him as if he had already quit and was no longer part of the organization where he had spent a large portion of his career. It helps if you feel you are retiring "to" something rather than "from" something.

Those who retire in this century have an added challenge. They'll probably have to subsidize about 10 to 15 percent of their income by part-time employment. That may not be as bad as it sounds, though. You might be able to turn a hobby into something that makes money. For example, if you've always enjoyed playing tennis, you could teach young people the skills of the game. You might also want to do something related to your current career. If you are a journalist for a local newspaper, you may decide to follow your dream of traveling and writing about your experiences in travel column or book. According to a number of national surveys, more than 80 percent of Baby Boomers intend to continue working at least part-time after their retirement.

The post-war generations have had to think through how they look at material things. Deena Katz, a financial advisor from Florida, has enunciated clearly the difference between the Boomers and their parents, who are often called the "Depression Generation." She wrote:

> The big issue for Baby Boomers is that they live in the present. . . . They have always given themselves everything they thought they were entitled to. When my folks needed a refrigerator, they saved money and bought it. Notice I said NEEDED, not wanted. Now, when boomers want a refrigerator, they buy it and pay it off over time. So the boomers are absolutely going to have a hard time adjusting to a downsized lifestyle because they haven't saved enough to continue as they have been living.[1]

Strategies for a comfortable retirement

Through using the following retirement strategies, Baby Boomers can greatly reduce the problems posed by lack of preretirement planning:

1. Identify your retirement goals

You'll probably find this to be the easiest part of planning for your future. Yet the average American adult spends less than ten hours per year planning for retirement, as compared to more than 145 hours shopping. This is the fun part of planning for retirement. This is where you can dream. Where do you want to retire? When do you want to retire? What do you want to do in your retirement? Sit down with your spouse and develop a list of what you want your retirement years to include. The answers to these questions will change during each decade of your life. In the last ten years before retirement, you will need to become more specific and realistic with your plans.

2. Develop a plan

Start by analyzing your current financial position. Ask yourself, "Are my present retirement goals realistic?" If they are, select the best strategies you can use to accomplish these goals. It may mean tightening your household budget, managing your savings and investments better, or participating in tax-sheltered annuities and IRAs if you are self-employed.

Now the hardest step: Follow through with a written action plan. Once you've implemented your action plan, monitor it annually to keep the numbers current. (Various financial changes such as changing interest rates may necessitate your recalculating the numbers so you can accurately predict whether you need to make changes to reach your goals.)

3. Figure your income

The financial services industry—stockbrokers, mutual fund companies, national and local banks, credit unions, and money magazines—continue to push the idea that for you to support yourself in retirement at the level of your current lifestyle, you'll need 70 to 80 percent of your preretirement income. These unrealistic projections have frightened individuals into frantic saving or putting off retirement. People choose not to deal with the issue because they don't know how.

Don't be alarmed by those percentages. There are many ways to lower living expenses. Some are as simple as moving to another state or to a more rural area with a less complicated lifestyle. In an April 2003 survey conducted for Del Webb, a major retirement community builder found that 59 percent of Baby Boomers aged forty-four to fifty-six plan to relocate when they retire. This is double the number of people in that age group who answered the same way in a survey in 1990.

Several Web sites provide data for retirees wanting to relocate to a less expensive location. Among them are <www.RetirementLiving.com> and <www.BestPlaces.net>—a site that gives some particularly good news. New Yorkers who make $100,000 per year would need only about 42 percent of their current income to maintain a comparable lifestyle if they relocate in Jacksonville, Florida, or Tucson, Arizona.

Keep in mind that the comparisons publicized by the financial services industry don't take into account changes in one's standard of living. They base their projections on *preretirement income,* whereas you need to design your life's final chapter on *postretirement expenses.* Mutual-fund companies and stockbrokers often fail to consider that if you move to a lower-cost area, the cost of housing drops by 60 to 70 percent; you probably no longer have children to shelter, feed and educate; you won't have employment-related expenses for such items as clothing, travel, and meals; and you'll have time to look for bargains and/or to produce you own goods, such as growing vegetables in a garden. You can live on much less than you think you can.

Another way to reduce expenses is to consider a move to a tax-friendly state. Currently, eight states have no state income tax—Alaska, Florida, Nevada, South Dakota, Tennessee, Texas, Washington, and Wyoming. Five other states have no sales tax—Alaska, Delaware, Montana, New Hampshire, and Oregon.

4. Retire your mortgage before you retire

Many Baby Boomers who have married and purchased homes in their late thirties or early forties will be saddled with mortgage payments into their seventies. Don't even think of retiring until you have burned that house mortgage. You can't afford to be paying a fixed expense like a home mortgage in retirement. If you are less than fifteen years from retirement, consider the following ways to pay off your mortgage sooner, possibly allowing you to retire sooner.

Pay more on the principal. In addition to your regular monthly mortgage payment, pay an extra amount. By doing so, you can reduce your mortgage by years and save tens of thousands of dollars in interest payments. For example, if you have a $100,000 loan for thirty years at 8 percent interest and you send your finance company an additional $100 payment each month, you'll reduce the life of your mortgage by ten years. You'll also save $64,000 in mortgage interest. If $100 is too much for you currently, start with just $20 per month. Even that small amount will make a dramatic difference. You'll shave off approximately three years from the life of your loan and save $20,000.

Change to a fifteen-year mortgage. Many people think that if they select a fifteen-year fixed mortgage, their monthly payments will double. But the new payments won't be anywhere near doubled. Usually, the change won't be much more than an extra 30 percent. For example, a $100,000, fifteen-year mortgage at 8 percent interest will cost $955 per month, compared to $733 per month—the cost of a thirty-year mortgage for the same amount at the same interest rate. With lower home-mortgage interest rates, you may be able to do even better. You may need to do a little belt-tightening at the beginning, but with cost-of-living raises or promotions, within a few years that extra won't seem like much.

Make payday mortgage payments. If your budget requires a thirty-year mortgage and you are paid every two weeks, use a "payday" mortgage. (Even if you are paid once a month, careful budgeting will allow you to implement this plan.) Instead of making a monthly mortgage payment, you make one every two weeks—often called a biweekly payment. Then, more of the payment is applied to the principal, and your equity in the home accrues faster.

Sometimes you can get this service free. If your lending institution wants to charge you $300 or more to set this up, you can avoid the charge and achieve the same goal by adding an extra payment annually. Making the equivalent of one extra full payment per year will shorten the term of the mortgage by almost eight years.

5. Reduce transportation costs

Scientists have ascertained that the universe contains many black holes—objects in space created by the collapse of a massive star. Their intense gravitation pulls in anything that gets too close; it's actually so strong that not even light can escape. Do you have a car, truck, or SUV that is a "black hole"—one that, ever since you bought it, seems to suck the life out of your finances in depreciation, maintenance, repairs, and daily travel expenses? Very old vehicles that constantly need repairs may do the same thing. The good news is that your vehicles don't have to do that to you. Here are some things you can do to save money on your vehicle:

Purchase the right type of vehicle. Before you fall in love with that sporty two-door roadster or that SUV, ask, "What am I going to use this vehicle for? Will I be driving it to the local store twice a week? Will I use it to transport my ten grandchildren to Disney World?"

Avoid depreciation. Unless you're planning to keep your vehicle for at least ten to twelve years, purchasing a new one makes no sense. By the time you drive it off the dealer's lot, you've lost from $3,000 to $5,000 on a midsize vehicle. Choose instead a two-year-old vehicle with fifteen thousand to twenty thousand miles on it. It still has at least fifteen thousand miles under the manufacturer's warranty.

Pay attention to maintenance. In retirement, you may have time to do some of your car's routine maintenance yourself. If you maintain your vehicle, you'll minimize the amount of repairs it needs. Recognize that both maintenance and repairs will increase as your automobile ages.

Reduce the number of vehicles you own. After retirement, the average cost of transportation drops 45 percent because you no longer have to make the daily drive to work. If you have limited transportation needs, you can choose to lower your costs even more by paring down to only one vehicle if you have more than one or by renting a vehicle one or two days a month and doing all your errands on that day. According to the American Automobile Association, the average family vehicle costs approximately $6,000 a year when you calculate in depreciation, gas, insurance, repairs, etc. That adds up.

6. Save regularly and early

Saving is not as hard as it seems, but it does demand action—the earlier the better, as the following illustration indicates. If your goal is to have $300,000 in the bank when you retire at age sixty-five, the best age to begin is twenty-five. If you contribute $200 per month until you're thirty, you'll have saved $12,000. If you don't save another cent, assuming an annual interest rate of 8 percent, you'll reach your retirement financial goal. If you wait until you're thirty-five, you'll have to make those $200 per month contributions until you're fifty, and you'll have contributed $36,000. If you begin to save the same monthly amount at age forty-five, you'll have to save nearly $65,000 over the next twenty-seven years to acquire the same $300,000.

However, it doesn't matter whether your retirement date is forty years or fifteen years in the future or whether you've already retired. Having a savings plan is essential for your financial well-being. Here are five saving strategies that will get you started.

Develop a plan. It's really hard to save money—unless you have a plan. Write down your goals and dreams that require financial planning. Planning for your future retirement should be a top priority on your list. Other dreams could include Christian education for your grandchildren, taking a mission trip or vacation overseas, or being totally debt-free from credit card or other loans within a specified time. Once you've listed these financial goals, prioritize them, price them, and set a realistic time to accomplish each one. To boost your motivation to save, post a picture of your dream home or a travel magazine scene of that foreign country you wish to visit—maybe even in your wallet right next to your credit card.

Don't delay. Financial counselors are always telling their clients to start saving early. The reasoning should be clear from this example: If you started investing $2,000 per year at age twenty-five at an average 8 percent rate of return, forty years later you'd have more than $606,000 in the bank. However, if you delay saving until you're thirty-five and then began to invest $2,000 annually at the same 8 percent interest rate, you'd have only $266,000 at age sixty-five.

Maybe you started out with good intentions but weren't able to stick to it. Don't be discouraged. It's never too late to save. An acquaintance of mine procrastinated saving for retirement. When he had only fifteen years to retirement, he hadn't saved one cent. So, during the next fifteen years, he took out his annual cost of living raise, saving fifty percent for his financial future and fifty percent for daily living increases. Just by setting aside that small amount, he accumulated more than $100,000 during those fifteen years.

Save unexpected income. Perhaps a relative left you some money in a trust, or you received an unexpected gift of money from a parent. Or maybe you can develop your own "unexpected" resource by having a garage sale and collecting $300 to $500 for your throw-away items. Or think of the annual tax refund—over the past five years, the average American family has received approximately $1,500 in tax refunds from the IRS. If you were to receive that amount annually and put it into savings, it would amount to more than $60,000 over an average working lifetime, or more than $22,000 if you started saving at age fifty. If you add the magic of compounding interest, your $60,000 or $22,000 would more than double.

Save from expected sources. You're probably saying to yourself, "I don't have any expected sources of extra income, and if I did, I have many other needs that it would have to go for before putting any into a savings account." The truth is that the majority of us *do* have expected sources of income. Take, for example, the vehicle you're driving. If you're like most people, you purchased it with a small down payment and then agreed to pay off the remainder of the cost in monthly installments. What will you do with the extra $400 per month you'll have once you've paid for the vehicle? Usually, people just let that extra $400 disappear into the expenses of daily living. However, if you start paying yourself that $400, putting it into a savings or investment account, your financial picture will be significantly helped in another four years.

Use direct deposit. The easiest method to save money is to have a set amount deducted each pay period from your salary or your social security deposit. This amount is then automatically transferred to your bank or credit union savings account, IRA, etc. The payday deduction is one of the reasons Europeans save at least seven times more than Americans do and the Japanese save ten times more. Most of us would be better off with this type of "forced" savings. Remember: What you don't see, you don't miss, and, better still, you don't spend!

7. Consider other income sources

Find out what your Social Security payment will be. When the national Old Age, Survivors, and Disability Insurance (OASDI), commonly known as Social Security, was enacted in 1935, the average male was expected to live twelve years beyond retirement. Currently, he can expect to live an additional fifteen to twenty years. Many people plan to depend on Social Security to cover 100 percent of their retirement living expenses, forgetting that it was designed to provide only for the basics—shelter, food, clothing, and utilities—not for home mortgages, vacations, and insurance.

Since now there are only three workers per every retiree as compared to thirty-five workers per retiree when Social Security began, the benefits for the Baby Boomers are not going to be the same as they are for today's seniors. In this century, Social Security benefits should account for approximately 40 percent of the average retiree's retirement income. However, don't assume you'll never be able to take advantage of this important program. According to the 2003 report from the Social Security trustees, the projected point at which tax revenues will fall below expenses will be 2018, and the trust fund won't be exhausted until around 2042.

To make sure you'll receive the benefits due to you, complete a Request for Earnings and Benefit Estimate Statement (Form SSA-7004) every three years. You can order a free copy of this form by calling 1-800-772-1213. You'll receive a statement of your earnings—according to their records—along with a projection of your future benefits. If the earning figures don't match those on your income tax returns, notify the Social Security Administration of the discrepancies.

Take advantage of employee and pretax programs. If your employer offers you any of the following retirement programs—401(k), 403(b), 457, or any other programs—take full advantage of them, because they are one of the best ways to save for retirement. Along with these pretax contributions, your employer may make a matching contribution. Unfortunately, many employees—up to 75 percent in some organizations—fail to take advantage of these programs. Over a forty-year working career, this could mean a retirement financial loss of more than $200,000. It is crucial that you do not delay saving for retirement. The best method is to arrange to have automatic withdrawals taken from your paycheck.

About investing

People often ask financial educators and planners, "How do I grow my investments whether I am still working or have already retired?" We'll cover some of the basic principles of investing that will help you work with your broker or develop your own portfolio for retirement. Before you set up your family or individual investment strategies, keep these two principles in mind: First, eliminate all consumer debt. This includes furniture and vehicle loans, as well as credit and charge accounts. Over one hundred years ago, Ellen White wrote, "With economy you may place something at interest. With wise management you can save something after paying your debts."[2] Second, set up an emergency account containing at least $1,000. This provides for unexpected financial emergencies such as car repairs and house maintenance items, thus removing the need to stack up credit-card debt.

There is a plethora of books about financial planning. One of them may surprise you: the Bible. Did you know that the Bible actually gives some important investment principles? Here are seven of those biblical guidelines:

1. Plan wisely

"The wise plan ahead and save for the days to come, but stupid people spend money as fast as they get it" (Proverbs 21:20, TCW). "Steady plodding brings prosperity" (Proverbs 21:5, TLB). In the original Hebrew, the phrase "steady plodding" implies someone who is filling a bucket one cup at a time. The investment that best represents this principle is your home. If you are wise, you will regularly add to your monthly mortgage payment and thereby pay off your home mortgage in a third to half the time of its term. If you do that, you'll save tens of thousand of dollars.

2. Diversify

Financial planners often stipulate that owning stocks over the long term will give you a better return. However, you may have only a short time to invest before retirement. Hence, you need a portfolio consisting of a variety of investments. Use stocks and mutual funds for long-term growth and certificates of deposit and treasury bills for short-term needs as your shelter against inflation. When it comes to investment advice, King Solomon was correct when he said, "Invest your money in seven places or even eight because you don't know what will fail and what will succeed" (Ecclesiastes 11:2, TCW).

3. Avoid speculation

Particularly when it comes to speculation, this golden rule applies: No matter how good the market looks, never invest money you can't afford to lose. If you read an article that says you should put all your money in one particular stock because it's going to go through the ceiling, it's time to be skeptical. "There is another serious problem I have seen everywhere—savings are put into risky investments that turn sour, and soon there is nothing left to pass on to one's son. The man who speculates is soon back to where he began—with nothing" (Ecclesiastes 5:13-15, TLB). Proverbs says, "Hasty speculation brings poverty" (21:5, TLB).

4. Timing

Many investors try to time the stock or bond market, hoping to sell when the market is high and buy again when stocks bottom out. If that worked, we could all be wealthy. It's not that simple though. Smart investors will always remember that time is their greatest asset. They won't let sudden market changes shake them up, and they won't be caught in impulse buying. "There are other things I've learned about life. There are times to do specific things and different seasons in which to do them" (Ecclesiastes 3:1, TCW).

5. Types of investing

Christians should avoid investing in the stocks and mutual funds of companies that profit from services and products that do not glorify God or that harm others. Because we believe that our bodies are temples of God, we need to stay clear of companies that destroy health or promote intemperance. Examples would be the tobacco and alcohol industries. "Dear friends, let us purify ourselves from everything that contaminates body and spirit" (2 Corinthians 7:1, NIV). "Woe to him who gives drink to his neighbors. . . . You will be filled with shame instead of glory" (Habakkuk 2:15, 16, NIV).

Obviously, in choosing an investment portfolio, we should also bypass those businesses that are involved in immoral and unethical practices. These could include gambling, weapons manufacturing, third-world sweatshops, abortion, and the pornographic entertainment industry, among others. The psalmist says, "You created my inmost being; you knit me together in my mother's womb. I praise you because I am fearfully and wonderfully made" (Psalm 139:13, 14). "Among you there must not be even a hint of sexual immorality, or of any kind of impurity . . . these are improper for God's holy people" (Ephesians 5:3).

Investing in socially conscious funds is one way to avoid working with the devil. Christians can't afford the short-lived profits gained by investing money in companies that may promote the eternal loss of precious souls for whom Jesus died.

6. Place your confidence in the Lord

Because only God can see the future, it pays to ask for His guidance in how you should invest. He will bless those who put their confidence and trust in Him. He will bless your efforts to become financially responsible. "Charge members who are rich not to become proud nor trust in their wealth. They should put their trust in God" (1 Timothy 6:17, TCW).

7. Give generously

God has given some the ability to make wise investments. He does this so that they may give of their accumulating wealth to spread the gospel and to provide for those in need. "They should focus their lives on doing good, becoming rich in virtue, helping those in need and being kind to everyone. This is like putting money which will never be devalued, in the bank of heaven. They'll have a life that's meaningful here, and in the end, they'll be given eternal life" (1 Timothy 6:18, 19, TCW).

Part-time employment

In the past, most individuals and families felt quite secure with Social Security, a pension, and some personal savings; but in the future, the majority of Americans will have to add a fourth leg to their retirement stool—a job. This might not be all bad. We have a tendency to see financial planning for retirement through society's eyes rather than biblical eyes. God's message to Adam and ultimately the whole human race was, "By the sweat of your brow you will eat your food until you return to the ground" (Genesis 3:19).

In fact, a recent study by Harvard University proves the importance of employment. The study involved two groups of one hundred Harvard graduates between the ages of sixty-five and seventy-five. The first group retired at age sixty-five, while the other group continued to work for another ten years. The results are a warning for those whose purpose in retirement is a life of ease and pleasure. Among those who retired at sixty-five, seven out of eight were dead by age seventy-five. Among those who continued to work, only one out of eight was dead by age seventy-five.

Contrary to popular opinion, creating a healthy financial plan for retirement does not have to be an unpleasant experience. In fact, after applying the above principles, you may discover the task to be both pleasant and rewarding, providing you with the monetary resources you'll need to fulfill your retirement dreams.

HOMEWORK

1. What are your financial goals for the future?
2. Make a budget covering your income and financial needs. (See the example below.)

Resources:

Fred Brock. *Retire on Less Than You Think*. New York: Times Books, 2004.

Robert Otterbourg. *Retire & Thrive*. Washington, D.C.: Kiplinger Books, 2003.

Concepts from *The Stewpot* articles, March and April 1998. Reprinted in *Ministry*, June 2001, April 2002.

Developing a Realistic Budget

If at retirement you find that you don't have the typical income of 70 percent of what you have been living on previously, don't despair. As pointed out in this chapter, you can live on approximately 40 percent of your working income. Maybe the following monthly budget will give you some financial hope:

Expenses

	Suggested Budget	Your Budget
Tithe and offerings	$400	$_____
Housing (property tax, maintenance, etc.)	$300	$_____
Household supplies (groceries, pet food, laundry, cleaning products, etc.)	$400	$_____
Clothing (dry cleaning, etc.)	$200	$_____
Vehicle (gas, maintenance, registration)	$300	$_____
Utilities (electricity, gas, water, etc.)	$300	$_____
Telephone (cell phone, Internet, TV, etc.)	$200	$_____
Medical (pharmacy, optical, dental)	$500	$_____
Insurance (house, vehicle, other, etc.)	$300	$_____
Gifts and hobbies	$100	$_____
Vacations	$200	$_____
Entertainment	$100	$_____
Miscellaneous	$200	$_____
Total	**$3,500**	$_____

Note: This budget assumes home ownership and a new or near-new vehicle paid for at retirement.

Income

Husband's Social Security	$1,100
Wife's Social Security	$900
Husband's and wife's mutual funds	$1,000
Part-time employment	$500
Total	**$3,500**

Planning Your Retirement Income

It is like a four-legged stool:

1. Social Security	30–40%
2. Pension, 401(k), 403(b), IRA, etc.	30–40%
3. Other income (rental, CDs, Roth)	10–15%
4. Part-time job	10–15%
Total	**100%**

1. Fred Brock, *Retire on Less Than You Think: The New York Times Guide to Planning Your Financial Future* (New York: Times Books, 2004), 18.

2. Ellen G. White, *Selected Messages* (Hagerstown, Md.: Review and Herald, 1958), 2:329.

CHAPTER

Intellectual Health

George Brown, age eighty, is a retired church executive. Looking at George, one would think he's in his late sixties. He's the epitome of good health—fit and trim, with a pleasant, heartwarming smile. There's a reason for George's youthful appearance. He says, "I make health a priority in my life. It is essential to me." It's clear that he's physically fit. What is less apparent is his continual quest to enrich his mind. To George, intellectual health is just as important as physical health.

Retirement gave George time to write that he didn't have when he was working full time. He wrote his first book when he was seventy. It sold more than 130,000 copies. The following year he was challenged to write another book, one about the fruit of the Spirit. It sold 70,000 copies. Writing was a life-long dream that George finally realized because he kept his mind continually active after he retired. He didn't gear down intellectually for retirement. Instead, he geared up. He shared his wisdom, a lifetime of learning, and his life experiences with a multitude of people through his books.

Even though George is now in his eighties, he still teaches a Bible class in his church every week. He also travels extensively for speaking appointments. And no matter where he is, he still walks regularly—three miles a day. George's enthusiasm is contagious. He says, "I'm still looking forward. . . . I want to make hay while the sun is shining." He's a prime example of someone who is enjoying an excellent quality of life.

To maintain quality of life as we age, we must maintain a healthy intellect. Many people whose bodies are showing age still have healthy minds and enjoy a high quality of life. "It is cognitive capacity, more than any physical disability, that most often determines whether people can attain extreme old age while remaining active. . . . No one achieves extreme old age without retaining a great deal of cognitive ability for most of his or her life."[1] If your mind is sharp and active, you can compensate for decline of physical ability. However, the reverse is not true. If your body is strong and healthy and your mind deteriorates significantly, your quality of life will be seriously diminished. This underlines the importance of maintaining your intellectual health.

This chapter will not deal with the issues of dementia, including Alzheimer's disease. If you want more information on these issues, you'll find it in the many books that have been written to deal with specific types of dementia along with their physical and mental implications. Here, we will focus on eliminating factors that may increase your risk of mental decline and suggest some ways you can enhance your long-term intellectual health.

Older people experience a huge range of health—from very poor to excellent. Perhaps the most drastic health differences in any one particular age group are in the areas of physical and intellectual health. When considering physical health, people who are sixty-five may be wheelchair bound or, conversely, having the time of their life playing tennis twice a week. The range of possibilities for a sixty-five-year-old's intellectual abilities is just as broad. Some of them gave up trying to expand their intellectual horizons years before. For them the sun has already set. Others are gearing up for the time of their lives. For them, the sun is still rising. Even in retirement, they feel they don't have enough time to learn it all.

Consider Jim, ninety-four, and Isabel, eighty-five. Jim and Isabel have a very healthy lifestyle that includes walking, a healthy diet, and church attendance every week. They share a walk every evening because they don't have time during the day. What is it that keeps a ninety-four-year-old and an eighty-five-year-old busy all day? Jim replies, "I write music every day to send to my publisher." Jim has his Ph.D. in music education. Isabel is also an educator in the field of music. Both of them enjoy attending concerts. Jim and Isabel are still benefiting others with the God-given musical talents they developed through a lifetime of education and use.

Intellectual decline

What about the intellectual decline often associated with aging? Many older people fear losing their mental faculties. It is common knowledge that some decline in mental function occurs after the age of sixty. However, there is good news: "Healthy older adults show no decline, and perhaps improve in some cognitive skills such as wisdom, judgment, creativity, common sense, coordination of facts and ideas, and breadth of knowledge and experience."[2]

Generally, intellectual decline associated with aging is limited to the areas of processing new information and retrieving old information. You may begin to process new information a little more slowly and retrieve information stored in your memory more slowly than earlier in life. The good news is that for the vast majority of people, everyday activities do not exceed cognitive capacities.

Just as people have more risk of developing cancer or heart disease in their sixties and seventies, so there is more risk for a decline in intellectual health. Focus on what you can do intellectually, not on what you can't do. Don't compare yourself to others around you. Start where you are, and maintain what you have while making improvements.

Some people become couch potatoes when they retire. They're physically inactive, lounging on the couch and watching TV. They start to decline physically because they rarely move from the couch. People who allow their minds to vegetate are couch potatoes of another sort. What are you willing to settle for intellectually?

The trend in our society is for people to accept information passively, without processing it. Media outlets such as TV and newspapers are especially conducive to this bad habit. Many people like to sit back and accept the crumbs of intellectual stimulation because it is easier than working to retain and apply the information themselves. If that describes you, stop putting yourself on the intellectual sidelines. You are limiting your enjoyment of the best years of your life. Don't allow yourself to become an unthinking quasi-intellectual.

Jesus told a story about a field: how the farmer must plow it, plant it, carefully tend it, and harvest it. Your mind is like a field. Preparing your mind to receive and process information corresponds with plowing. When you take care of your body, your mind will work better. Get enough sleep, exercise, eat healthfully.

The next step is to plant seeds. The seeds are your thoughts, your dreams for the future, and the mind-stretching activities in which you engage. Put yourself in situations where you will need to use your brain. Do crossword puzzles; take a class; read an intellectually stimulating book. Don't be a passive receptacle for information. Process that information and use it to expand the knowledge you already have. Apply it to your life. What you harvest depends on what you plant.

After you plant the seeds, you can't just ignore them. Weeds will grow faster than the good plants if you don't get rid of them. Carefully tend to your crop by dealing with the weeds of fear, anxiety, and negative assumptions that enter the mind, threatening the seeds you have planted.

The result of your hard work is the harvest. Not only will you have access to more information, but you will also have more wisdom. Your mind will be more active and healthy, and your quality of life will be enhanced. The intellectual harvest takes place throughout life—including the retirement years.

There is a way that seems easier. You can plow a field and let it go, not planting, not cultivating, and then come back at the end of the growing season to find the field growing with nothing but weeds. You don't have to work to acquire weeds. However, they won't produce a harvest; you won't have any benefits to reap. A field of weeds is an eyesore, a waste of good land. And the mind is indeed a terrible thing to waste.

Intellectual advantages of growing older

When do you reach your intellectual peak? Physically, twenty-year-olds are at their peak. That's early in life. However, you may not reach your intellectual peak until you're in your fifties or even sixties. Some even produce their greatest intellectual achievements in their seventies or later. That is only the case for those who continue to keep their minds active. There are those who never progress intellectually past the age of fifteen or sixteen. They drop out of school and never read another book the rest of their lives. They settle for intellectual crumbs.

On the other hand, some university professors are doing their best teaching in their seventies. Some of the best books ever written are by authors between the ages of sixty-five and seventy-five. They're writing from the perspective of a lifetime of work, study, and experience in their field. We know Moses, an intellectual giant, for what he accomplished after age eighty.

During your lifetime, you've faced many challenges. You've weathered many changes, such as those brought on by new technology that changes the way we live. Society itself changes. As these changes occur, you comprehend more about life, about what is important, about human needs, and about adjusting successfully to life's new form. We call that wisdom. Usually, wisdom brings more personal fulfillment. Perhaps your memory is a little weaker and your learning process a little slower, but you can compensate for that with wisdom. It's an important component of quality of life.

You have an opportunity to use your wisdom within your family—not to push your ideas onto your children or grandchildren, which is a misuse of wisdom, but to be there as a wise family member who has traveled the road already. Grandchildren may look to grandparents for ideas, support, and sometimes even counsel. The wisdom you've accumulated throughout your life will help those who ask for your advice. It will enable them to make sound decisions.

In addition to helping your friends and family, as you develop more wisdom, you may have the opportunity to make an impact in your church through mature leadership. Wisdom is needed in community organizations, service clubs, and schools. Don't stay on the sidelines. Become actively engaged with your family, community, and church.

Another benefit of mature years is the ability to make good judgments. Younger people may be more energetic, but they are sometimes greater risk-takers or more compulsive about their decisions. Older people have learned from some of their mistakes and can make better decisions because of their good judgment.

Risk factors for intellectual health

Just as there are risk factors that contribute to poor physical health, so there are risk factors that contribute to poor intellectual health. Let's look at ten risk factors that may impede optimal intellectual health and some ways to avoid or eliminate those risk factors through preventive health care.

1. Genetics

Genetic factors affect capacity and function in varied degrees, depending on the task. Though you were born with a certain capacity for intellectual development, you can still greatly affect your intellectual health through controlling environmental factors and maintaining a positive attitude. It also helps to refrain from comparing yourself to others. You'll always find someone who is smarter, faster, or more creative. Celebrate your talents. You are a unique individual. No one else has the same qualities you have. If you develop the intellectual talents you have, you're far better off than people with an IQ of 180 who have stopped using their brains.

2. Cardiovascular disease

Cardiovascular disease is not only the leading cause of death in America but also a major risk factor for cognitive decline as one ages. Atherosclerosis and hardening of the arteries contribute to hypertension and strokes. Strokes of any nature, whether small or large, may damage a person's cognitive abilities. Heart disease and hypertension also precipitate cognitive decline.

If heart disease runs in your family or you know you are at risk for other reasons, see your doctor and ask about preventive measures you can take to reduce your risk. The previous two chapters cover this subject too. Proper diet, exercise, and weight are particularly important to prevent poor intellectual health.

3. Lack of friendships

Another risk factor for intellectual decline is a lack of close friendships. Compared to people with no social ties, those with five or six close friends were 2.4 times less likely to experience cognitive decline over a twelve-year period.[3] Develop the friendships you have and seek out new friends. Find people to talk to who share some of your interests. Conversation will keep your brain working. Even more importantly, when you feel you are accepted, your life will have more meaning.

4. Low self-efficacy

Self-efficacy is crucial in maintaining intellectual well-being. Self-efficacy is your belief in your ability to do something. When you have low self-efficacy, you say, "I don't think I can do that." The old saying "use it or lose it" is an important factor here. When people become doubtful or fearful about their ability to do things, they stop doing those things. That causes their quality of life to deteriorate. Remember at the very beginning of the book when we talked about how assumptions determine behavior? That is related to self-efficacy. Here is an example of someone with low self-efficacy. Assumption: *I think I can't take this class—I won't be able to comprehend the concepts.* Behavior: The person doesn't take the class. Result: He misses the opportunity to stretch his brain. Such progressions can start a downward spiral. The less people do, the less they think they can do, and so it goes.

Joe, an older volunteer at the hospital where I worked, had always wanted to go to college but had never had the opportunity. In spite of his age, he took college classes until he graduated at the age of eighty. He was very proud of his accomplishment. That is an example of high self-efficacy. You can either go for it like Joe or give up. Don't give up. Stretch your brain.

5. Depression and anxiety

Depression can cause a number of problems that impair intellectual function. These include poor memory, a slowing of the thinking processes, inability to concentrate, and problems making decisions. Depression is a risk factor for both cognitive decline and dementia.[4] It leads to negative thinking—to focusing on problems and the negative aspects of life. The chapter in this book on emotional health covers depression more fully.

Anxiety is a diagnosis that many times accompanies depression. It may interfere with cognitive abilities because excessive worry and preoccupation with potential dangers crowd the mind. The best way to deal with depression or anxiety that in any way affects your normal function is to see a mental-health professional.

6. Impaired sensory function

Declining sight, hearing, taste, touch, and smell limit both the quantity and quality of information that you receive. This is obviously a risk factor to intellectual health as well as to quality of life. Most of these conditions are treatable by quality health care. Don't just accept any of these conditions as a part of growing older. You may be accepting a lowered quality of life unnecessarily.

If you do suffer a sensory handicap that can't be completely cured medically, don't back away from enjoying life and interacting with people. Learn to compensate for the decline in function; learn a new way to do what you enjoy doing. Take Dr. Steen, for instance. Though this missionary physician's eyesight is failing, he is serious about retaining his intellectual health. He uses adaptive equipment to enhance what remaining eyesight he has so he can keep on learning and functioning. He won't let the world pass him by.

7. Stress

Stress is a part of life at any age. Many look forward to retirement as a time to get away from stress and the pressures of life. However, as you age, you will experience new stressors. For example, when you retire, health-related stressors may replace job-related stressors. Research studies show that a continual exposure to stress accelerates the decline in cognitive ability.[5] Stress at any age can lower your ability to think clearly. However, by dealing with the stress you face, you can lessen its negative impact on you. We'll take a more extensive look at stress in the chapter on emotional health.

Let's enjoy life by following the blueprint that God gave us. That doesn't include trying to stuff two days' worth of work into one day. Reducing stress means taking a hard look at your lifestyle. Are you too busy to enjoy each day? You may have to change either your day-to-day activities or the way you respond to the pressures of life. The principles of reducing stress are not age-specific. The same techniques work whether you are fifteen or ninety-five. Even when you no longer have a formal job, your life can easily become unbalanced. Make sure you arrange for enough time for rest and relaxation. Don't overcommit yourself. Learn to say no. Overcommitting can lead to feeling overwhelmed and stressed-out.

Perhaps it is time for you to simplify your life. When you lower your level of stress, you will enjoy life more. That in turn will help you be healthier both mentally and physically.

8. Alcohol consumption

Alcohol is a problem for many older adults. Some abuse alcohol in an attempt to feel good despite their problems. Drinking alcohol brings its own set of problems. First, older people are more sensitive to the adverse effects of alcohol because of the age-related changes in their bodies. Second, alcohol can interact with medications, and older people tend to take more medications than do their younger counterparts. Third, alcohol contributes to depression, and depression may then lead to more alcohol consumption, creating a vicious cycle. Alcohol also directly affects the thinking process and people's judgment. For good intellectual health, it is best to avoid alcohol.[6]

9. Lack of formal education

The education you received when you were young is one of the strongest factors contributing to your intellectual health later in life. A college education contributes not only to better physical health but also to better memory and cognitive function as you get older.

If you are older and haven't reached the level of education you would have liked to have attained, it isn't too late. Many universities offer deeply discounted or even free classes to those over a certain age. Even if you don't want a formal degree, you can take continuing education classes at a local community college.

10. Negative emotions and thoughts

Negative emotions, such as guilt, anxiety, discontent, and distrust, all tend to break down a healthy mind. Especially when left unaddressed, these negative emotions may impede intellectual health. Make a conscious effort to banish negative thoughts and to replace them with positive ones. We will present further strategies to that end in the chapter on emotional health.

Prevention

Protecting your mind is just as important as protecting your body. Prevention for intellectual well-being involves becoming educated about the process and taking steps to eliminate or reduce risk factors that may be an issue for you. Taking steps toward better intellectual health will also help your health in other areas.

Here are three preventive measures you can take so you can experience prime-time aging for your mind:

1. Self-guided mental workouts

One of the best ways to keep your mind healthy is to keep it engaged in stimulating mental activities.[7] There are many ways to do this, from doing crossword puzzles to learning a second language to reading thought-provoking books or magazine or journal articles. Activities that require coordination of brain functions, like playing a musical instrument or painting pictures, benefit the brain in several ways. Playing the piano or another musical instrument involves hand-eye coordination, auditory input practice, and memorizing theory and musical sequences. This gives the whole brain a workout.

Writing is another activity that stimulates the brain. You may say, "I'm not a writer." That's OK. You don't have to write for publication to give your brain a workout. Some people write an auto-biography just for their families. The process stimulates the mind as they review life events, organize their thoughts, and then put words onto paper. It is a great form of creative expression available to everyone.

Mental activity is essential to keeping your mind functioning at peak capacity. Sometimes we're tempted to excuse mental laziness because of our age. We must practice self-discipline in learning or we find it too easy to become intellectual couch potatoes. "Learn-ing new things is the key to mental vigor. Learning stimulates the growth of dendrites and creates additional neuronal networks, which . . . appears to be important for overcoming damage to brain tis-sue."[8]

Caring for your mind has a strong spiritual basis. The apostle Paul wrote, "God hath not given us the spirit of fear, but of power and of love and of a sound mind" (2 Timothy 1:7). God wants you to have power and love and a sound mind. In Philippians 2:5, Paul said, "Let this mind be in you which was also in Christ Jesus" (KJV). What a thought—your mind can resemble the mind of Jesus!

2. Late-life learning

Never stop learning. Late-life learning helps preserve your cog-nitive abilities. No matter how old you are, you still have many opportunities to use your mind. Formal education is very afford-able for older people. Many public universities and community colleges offer special rates and special classes for older persons. Some people take just a class or two, while others enroll in degree pro-grams.

Elderhostel offers another type of learning experience that is slightly less structured. Elderhostel is an organization that uses re-tired college professors to teach classes—usually from one to two weeks in duration. Most of the classes are taught in conjunction with travel to locations relevant to the content. More than two thousand colleges and other institutions in fifty countries partici-pate in this program. At the time of the writing of this book, about 250,000 older individuals per year took an Elderhostel educational trip.

The easiest way to take a class is via the Internet. You can take college classes online without even leaving home. There are many other options available to enable you to engage in lifelong learning. Even if you choose not to take a formal class or degree program, use the events, people, and places around you to expand your mind. You can be creative even if you are in an isolated location with few resources at your disposal.

3. Exercise

Research studies show a significant association between physical activity level and cognitive health.[9] This is true of older adults who are physically active in either light, moderate, or strenuous exercise. Exercise is essential to keeping the body strong; but it is just as effective in keeping your brain healthy and strong.

While exercise is not the magic cure-all for everything, it certainly can help reduce or eliminate many physical and emotional risk factors for poor cognitive health, such as cardio-vascular disease and depression. It also helps you deal better with normal daily stress.

Intellectual prime-time aging

I received a birthday card this year that read, "How can I be going downhill? I never reached the top!" Perhaps you can identify with the words on that card. People don't like to feel they didn't reach their potential. Maybe you feel you have what it takes but that you never took the time or perhaps didn't have the opportunity to pursue your goals intellectually. It's not too late! Even in retirement you can get in touch with your dreams—better now than never. God is in the business of repairing broken dreams.

Let's look at the strengths of being older—you use your strengths, not your weaknesses, to succeed. These strengths include wisdom, knowledge, a lifetime of experiences, maturity, common sense, and good judgment. What a list! This is the payoff for living a long time. Don't sell yourself short on any of these assets. True, you may not have the wisdom of Solomon; you may not even have as much knowledge as you think you need to do what you want to do; and maybe some of your life experiences ended badly. However, you probably learned more from those mistakes than you would have from a whole barnful of successes. Life experience has given you maturity, the ability to think things through before you act. There's a lot to be said for that.

All these qualities add up to intellectual prime-time aging. When you add love, commitment, compassion, and time to all of the above qualities, you can make a huge difference in yourself and in those around you.

HOMEWORK

1. What kinds of things can you add to your life to expand your mind?
2. List some potential risk factors in your life that may impede good intellectual health for you.
3. Write down some ways you could help others with the intellectual abilities God has given you.

1. Thomas T. Perls, Margery Hutter Silver, and John F. Lauerman, *Living to 100: Lessons in Living to Your Potential at Any Age* (New York: Basic Books, 2000), 157.

2. Miller, 29.

3. Linda J. Ball and Stanley J. Birge, "Prevention of Brain Aging and Dementia," *Clinics in Geriatric Medicine* 18 (2002), 495.

4. Ibid., 490.

5. Ibid.

6. C. F. Hybels and D. G. Blazer, *Clinics in Geriatric Medicine* 19 (2003), 673.

7. Perls et al., 159.

8. Ibid., 150.

9. Ball and Birge, 495.

CHAPTER

Emotional Health

Retirement should be a time of happiness and contentment. It is a time to interact more fully with family and friends, to find fulfillment for long-dreamed dreams. For this to happen, we must have emotional health. This chapter focuses on issues related to our emotions that may impede our health and happiness and some things we can do to improve our emotional health. No matter how many things threaten our health and happiness, God can deal with them. He wants to heal our emotional wounds.

Emotional wounds
We'll begin this chapter by looking at emotional wounds and how we can help them heal. Later, we'll look at the positive components of emotional health.

1. Loneliness
One definition of loneliness is "the discrepancy between the desired and actual closeness of a relationship between persons." This helps explain why people can feel lonely in a marriage. Even in marriages involving retired spouses, loneliness can be an issue. We may have expectations regarding closeness or intimacy. When our relationships don't meet those expectations, we feel lonely. An important component of a happy retirement for married people is maintaining a happy and fulfilling rela-

tionship. A happy marriage contributes to a longer and happier life.

The book *Happiness Is a Choice* suggests three basic causes for the pain of loneliness: lack of self-worth—that is, a lack of intimacy with self; lack of intimacy with others; and lack of intimacy with God.[1] Considering these causes, let's look at ways to overcome loneliness with God's help.

With God's help, you can overcome loneliness. Make this your creed:

I consider myself a worthwhile individual, someone whom God loves. He made me with a unique personality, talents, and strengths. I appreciate the way God created me. I appreciate my uniqueness. I enjoy my own company. I spend time doing things I like to do.

I appreciate and accept the strengths and the uniqueness of others. Other people don't always have to agree with me— I understand that developing closeness with others involves appreciating their opinions and ideas. When I can truly love and accept other people, no matter what their weaknesses, I will experience the bonds of lasting friendships.

I will learn how to forgive others and myself. (See the section on forgiveness in this chapter.) I won't hold grudges against people. Grudges separate and isolate individuals from each other.

I will visualize myself as happy. I will think happy, pleasant thoughts. I will not dwell on negative thoughts, events, circumstances, or failures. Happy people attract friends. Sad, gloomy people drive people away. I will count the blessings God has given me—especially when I am tempted to be gloomy.

I won't try to overcome loneliness by superficial means. Such means include mind-altering substances such as alcohol or drugs or anything else that may become an excuse to avoid living to the fullest. Instead, I will look for the best things in my life and seek to enjoy whatever blessings God has in store for me.

I will spend time with God—the One who created me, the One who loves me. He desires a personal relationship with each of His children, and I am a child of His. I will develop an enduring and meaningful relationship with Him through prayer and Bible study.

2. Stress

Stress follows people all through life. Many people see retirement as a time when they won't have the pressures and stresses of the job, their children are independent, and they've paid off their mortgage. So they assume that they can kick back and enjoy a stress-free life. Unfortunately, new stressors replace the old ones.

What is stress, and what is a stressor? A stressor is an event, disturbance, or demand that causes stress. Stress is your body's response to the stressor. A stressor is having a flat tire en route to an appointment. Stress is your response to the stressor, the flat tire. For some people, the stress response is minimal. They stop, jack up the car, change the tire, jump back in, and drive down the road as if nothing had gone wrong. The worst part of the ordeal for them may be their dirty hands.

Other people react with a big stress response. The circumstances may be different. They may be late for an important appointment. Perhaps they are physically unable to change the tire. Maybe it's zero degrees outside, and they don't have a cell phone.

Stressors, too, vary in intensity. Experiences such as the death of a child, spouse, or parent are major stressors. Minor stressors may include losing electrical power for an hour because of a storm. Other stressors are what most people would consider moderate, but that people react to differently. Examples include dealing with the death of a friend or a chronic but nonlife-threatening condition, such as loss of hearing.

Some stressors are totally beyond our control; we can't do anything about them. Aging is such a stressor. For others, an uncontrollable stressor may be the new neighbor who has just moved in with a barking dog or noisy teenagers.

Then there are stressors over which you have some control. You have a certain degree of control over your health, for instance. You choose whether or not to exercise. You choose to eat good, nutritious food and to maintain a healthy weight. You put yourself at risk if you choose to live an unhealthy lifestyle.

You cannot eliminate all stressors from your life; they're part of daily living. However, you can learn some techniques to limit some of the stressors in your life and choose how you respond to the remaining stressors.

Adopt a healthy lifestyle. One of the most important ways to manage stress is to keep your body physically fit. The problem is that an aging body can be a major stressor. The solution is to keep your body in the best physical condition possible. If you're sick, stress can overwhelm the system, resulting in a serious illness.

Live an enjoyable and balanced life. Many people's lives are out of control, often due to job-related stress. Retired people have an advantage. Life no longer centers on a job. Even so, retirement living can get out of balance. Some retirees say they work harder after retirement than before. Others find themselves wondering about how to fill their time. Put enjoyable events in your daily schedule. This is the time for you to do those things you've always wanted to do.

Manage the change in your life. Too much change is a stressor—even if it is change for the better. If possible, avoid making a lot of changes all at once.

Learn to relax. You should be able to relax during your retirement years even if you couldn't before. Take time every day to sit back and do nothing. Don't try to squeeze too many projects into one day. What you don't complete today will still be there tomorrow. Relax with a good book, or sit and listen to some soothing music. Take a warm bath. Enjoy a beautiful sunrise or sunset.

Exercise daily. Physical activity helps relieve stress by relaxing the muscles, improving sleep, releasing endorphins (natural chemicals that help us feel good), and releasing pent-up feelings associated with stress.

Resolve conflicts. Life is too short to harbor grudges. Learn to forgive.

Give God your cares and anxiety. First Peter 5:7 reminds us to "cast all your anxiety on Him because He cares for you." We often feel we have to find a solution to all our problems. In actuality, God has the solution to all our problems.[2]

My cat Boots enjoys walking with me. She usually walks right behind me. However, if she spots a dog or some other perceived danger, she runs for cover. I tell her I'm there to protect her and that I will pick her up and carry her so that no dog will hurt her. But she will have none of that. She just doesn't trust me to protect her. She has to do it her way.

How like Boots I am! God wants to hold me in His arms. He wants to protect me, but like Boots, I run away because I like to do things my way. When I bring my stressors to God, though, He handles them. I don't need to be stressed out.

3. Anger

Anger is another major roadblock to emotional health. Wouldn't it be nice if you didn't have to deal with anger? Some people are uncomfortable even talking about it. You may not want to admit that you're angry. You might say, "I'm not angry; I'm only a little annoyed." We substitute many other words for the word *anger,* words that aren't quite as strong—*frustrated, irritable, irked, mad.*

At every stage of life, we have developmental tasks to master. For instance, two-year-olds need to learn to play beside each other happily. Picture two two-year-olds with two trucks. They both decide they want the same truck. They yank at it until the stronger one tugs it out of the other's hands. Not to be outdone, the loser hits and kicks the other. Picture, then, the mother excusing his anger by saying, "He's only two years old; it's OK."

If similar scenes are repeated with similar responses, the child won't learn to deal with his anger. When he's four years old and still hasn't learned how to control his anger, he'll continue to hit and kick. People will consider him a mean little boy. At seven years of age, if his anger is still uncontrolled, people will start to call him a bully. As an angry teenager, he'll get into trouble that is more serious and become a juvenile delinquent. When you don't learn a task when you should learn it, you continue to take that problem with you through the years, perhaps even into your old age. That boy may become an angry senior citizen. He's angry at "the system"—too angry to enjoy a happy retirement. To avoid spending your last years that way, you may need to play catch up and learn to deal with anger in a healthy way.

When anger prevents you from maintaining successful relationships, you have a problem. Anger affects all those around you, even those who are not the objects of your anger. It creates a poisonous environment that brings fear and worry into relationships.

How can you deal with anger? God gave us great advice: "Do not let the sun go down while you are still angry" (Ephesians 4:26). Deal with the anger now. Go to the person you are angry with and solve the problem in a positive, nonjudgmental way. Here are some steps to help you deal with anger:

Step 1: Recognize that you are becoming angry. Be in tune with your feelings, but don't feed them with more negative emotions.

Step 2: Pray. Ask God to help you get through the situation without harming yourself or the others involved.

Step 3: Ask yourself if your anger is legitimate. The answer might surprise you. Perhaps you don't have a legitimate reason to be angry. For example, you may feel angry at what another person said to you, but when you look at the situation a little more closely, you realize it was a simple misunderstanding. No one was really at fault. Or maybe you'll conclude that it was your own fault! You may discover that the situation doesn't merit being angry and holding a grudge.

Step 4: If necessary, determine a course of action. This may include talking with the other person or persons involved. It should include time praying about the situation and asking God for wisdom.

Step 5: Forgive and go on with life. However you choose to deal with your anger, don't forget the biblical advice: "In your anger do not sin" (Ephesians 4:26). When you are angry with someone, you are in greater danger of hurting that person and dishonoring God. Jesus said, "Blessed are the peacemakers, for they will be called sons of God" (Matthew 5:9). Live in peace, not in anger.

4. Depression

In the United States, nineteen million people suffer from depression. It is the most common mood disorder in this country. Up to 10 percent of the population suffer from at least some depression sometime during the year. For older adults that figure goes up to 20 percent.

Depression is a serious condition that can greatly lower quality of life. It affects nearly every area of a person's life—physical, social, intellectual, and spiritual. Smoking, alcohol, certain medications, lack of exercise, and a high level of stress are lifestyle issues that contribute to this condition.

Depression comes in a variety of forms. Situational depression is, as the name implies, caused by a particular situation, such as the death of a family member or friend, loss of a job, or absence of social support. At times, your emotional energy may simply be at low ebb, causing a "blue" day. You don't feel like your normal, happy self, but you can't quite figure out why.

Then there is major depression, a serious health condition. This condition needs assessment and treatment by a qualified and knowledgeable physician. Don't ignore the symptoms of depression. The consequences are significant. Not only does depression raise the risk of disability, it also raises the likelihood of a need for nursing-home care. In fact, admission to a nursing home is more likely because of poor mental health than poor physical health. It is a condition that can cause serious problems, no matter what your age.

The section that follows doesn't offer treatment for major, clinically defined depression. These suggestions are intended to alleviate the short-term, situational type of depression.

Good nutrition. While most everyone today recognizes the importance of a nutritious diet for the prevention of physical disease, many people are unaware of the role nutrition plays in mental health, particularly in preventing depression. The following nutritional considerations play a large role in your moods and overall mental state.

- *Protein.* The protein in food is made up of amino acids. Tryptophan is one of these amino acids. The brain uses tryptophan to make serotonin, which is an important neurotransmitter that helps regulate mood. When serotonin is abundant and active, your feelings of well-being are heightened. To make serotonin, the brain must have a good supply of tryptophan.

The following foods are good sources of tryptophan: tofu, sesame seeds, pumpkin seeds, almonds, black walnuts, soybeans, brown rice, and black-eyed peas.

- *Carbohydrates.* Carbohydrates are essential to the brain not only because the brain needs a constant supply of the glucose that all carbohydrates supply but also because a high-carbohydrate diet increases the brain's production of serotonin. It is important, however, to choose the healthy types of carbohydrates (unrefined, simple and complex). Examples are given in chapter 4 of this book.
- *B-complex vitamins.* Deficiencies of folic acid, B6, and B12 have also been linked to depression. These vitamins, plus thiamine, riboflavin, and niacin (also B vitamins) are important for nervous system functioning. Include dark green, leafy vegetables; bananas; avocados; and whole grains in your daily diet.
- *Essential fats.* Although too much of the wrong kind of fat can contribute to health problems, you do need to get the good kinds of fat. These are specifically the omega-3 fatty acids (for further explanation, see chapter 4). These essential fats have been found to help manage mood. Omega-3 fats are found especially in flaxseeds, flaxseed oil, walnuts, canola oil, spinach, almonds, and avocados.
- *Caffeine.* Caffeine overstimulates the nervous system and has the potential to raise anxiety levels. Very frequently, anxiety and depression go hand-in-hand; if your anxiety level is high, it may be more difficult to recover from depression.
- *Alcohol.* Alcohol acts as a depressant and can make depression worse. Many who are depressed rely on alcohol to help them "feel good." This not only creates a vicious cycle but also can cause deficiencies of the B vitamins necessary for good mental health.

Here is a summary of the nutritional changes that can help you get over short-term, situational depression: eat three nutritious meals a day; choose minimally processed, simple and complex carbohydrates; eat foods that provide omega-3 fats; avoid caffeine and alcohol; and drink plenty of water.

Exercise. Another easy solution to depression is exercise. Over a five-year period, Duke University Medical Center researchers studied 156 middle-aged to older persons who suffered from major depressive disorders. The participants were divided into three treatment groups: those who exercised, those who took medication, and those who both exercised and took medication. The exercise group walked thirty minutes, three times a week. (They had not been exercising before the study.) Sixteen weeks later, the research scientist evaluated each person and assessed his or her level of depression. The results for the exercise-only group were astounding: 60.4 percent were no longer depressed. Of those on medication alone, 65.5 percent were no longer depressed. Among those who combined exercise and medication, 68.8 percent were no longer depressed.

Wow! Walking just thirty minutes, three times a week offers nearly the same benefit as the traditional prescription drug approach to depression treatment. And it costs nothing and has no side effects! Now, people who want to take responsibility for their own health have an alternative to medications as a treatment for depression.* Antidepressants are not effective for almost one-third of depressed patients. This group now has another viable option.[3]

Restful sleep. "Mood is even more dramatically impaired by sleep deprivation than is physical performance. With 6 to 8 percent of the population suffering from depression . . . and a majority of Americans admitting that they don't get enough sleep, it's likely that better sleep habits could improve outlook and emotional health for many individuals."[4]

Most people need seven to eight hours of quality sleep each night, some even more. Quality sleep sharpens memory and mental function, raises mood, eases depressive feelings, and enhances the immune system. Many older people suffer from a lack of quality sleep. Here are some suggestions for improving the quality of your sleep:

------

*Please note that just as drugs may not be effective for everyone, so exercise alone may not be enough to alleviate your depression. Ask your doctor to help you devise a plan that best fits your needs.

- Go to bed at the same time every night, including weekends.
- Don't nap during the day.
- Avoid nicotine and caffeine.
- Don't eat late evening or night meals.
- Don't go to bed right after viewing television or participating in stressful activities.
- Exercise during the day but not immediately before going to bed.
- Take a warm bath or shower before going to bed.
- Don't drink liquids for several hours before bedtime to avoid having to go to the bathroom during the night.

Trust in God. Jesus invites, "Come to me, all you who are weary and burdened, and I will give you rest. Take my yoke upon you and learn from me, for I am gentle and humble in heart, and you will find rest for your souls" (Matthew 11:28, 29).

When your burdens are too heavy, when you are weary with life's burdens and trials, Jesus says, "Come to me. . . . I will give you rest." What a promise! What a comforting thought! This rest is for body, mind, and soul.

Forgiveness. Whatever your age, you have and will continue to face challenges in your interpersonal relationships. People you love sometimes fail you. Likewise, there are times you say or do things that hurt someone else. Usually a genuine "I'm sorry" is appropriate and solves the problem. The wronged person accepts the apology, and the issue is resolved. Unfortunately, some people find it difficult to say, "I'm sorry." They nearly always blame someone else for the problem. Others find it difficult to forgive hurts and let them pass.

Don't allow lack of forgiveness to ruin your life. Unforgiven incidents eat at your soul. So, forgive yourself for your past failures, and forgive others when they wrong you. Forgiving means letting go of the wrong that has been done to you. Don't seek to get even or hold a grudge.

In this world of conflict, war, abuse, family problems, poverty, and violence, only forgiveness can pave the way for peace. Do you desire peace strongly enough to do something about it? Are you willing to release your anger? Forgiveness is like breathing. You exhale the stale air of hurt, anger, and desire for revenge. You inhale the fresh air of God's love and forgiveness.

Forgiveness is necessary when you've been hurt. Think of people who have hurt you, people against whom you are holding a grudge. Perhaps you even wish something bad would happen to them. If this is the case, you need to forgive. You might have excused yourself for not forgiving them because the hurt is so intense. You think, *It wouldn't be fair to forgive; they need to pay for what they've done.* However, refusing to forgive punishes only you, not the people who have wronged you.

Jesus heals broken hearts. He knows what it means to be hurt. He knows what it means to be rejected, mistreated, and verbally and physically abused. The people He came to save nailed Him to a cross. When He was on that cross, the crowd taunted and jeered. Talk about something being unfair! Nothing in the history of the world has ever been more unfair. Yet, while Jesus was on the cross, He prayed, "Father, forgive them, for they do not know what they are doing" (Luke 23:34).

You say that you were treated unfairly, and because it is so personal, so unfair, and so painful, you can't forgive. How does the unfairness that Jesus, the Son of God, experienced compare to the unfairness you suffered? Jesus gave us the ultimate example of forgiveness. He came to this earth and was nailed to the cross specifically to forgive you and me, to give us healing from all our hurts.

God's way of dealing with sinners will bring reconciliation. It will restore broken, damaged relationships. That means you must relinquish retribution and revenge to God. When you do this, you allow God to solve the problem His way. You allow God's love to permeate your life. As you experience God's healing and forgiving love, you will become more willing and able to forgive those who hurt you.

A potpourri of healthy emotions

1. Love

The basis of good emotional health and happiness is love—God's love for you. John tells us, "God is love" (1 John 4:8). His love is unconditional. Jesus Christ exemplified this love when He was here on this earth. He reached out to hurting people wherever He went. Children and adults alike followed Him from hillside to lakeside to hear His words of peace and love. Whatever your needs are, Jesus invites you to come to Him so He can fill you with His love. He says, "Whoever comes to me I will never drive away" (John 6:37).

2. Hope

Philippians 1:6 says, "Being confident of this, that he [God] who began a good work in you will carry it on to completion until the day of Christ Jesus." What a statement of hope! You can have confidence that God has invested in you. You are His special project. He's going to complete in you the good work that He's begun. You can count on it!

Do you know that God Himself is a God of hope? You may want to copy this verse and put it on your mirror or refrigerator: "May the God of hope fill you will all joy and peace as you trust in him, so that you may overflow with hope by the power of the Holy Spirit" (Romans 15:13). Not only does God want you to have hope, He also makes it easily accessible to you. By the power of the Holy Spirit, He will give you this hope. Your life will overflow with it. In addition, you will be filled with joy and peace. This is God's promise to you.

3. Contentment

What is the secret to a contented life? Paul had it figured out. For him, it began with the concept of "forgetting what is behind" (Philippians 3:13). No, Paul was not losing his memory. He deliberately chose not to dwell on the past events of his life—whether good or bad. He had some great experiences, and he had some very stressful experiences (see 2 Corinthians 11:23-27). His secret for contentment was this: "I rejoice greatly in the Lord. . . . I have learned to be content whatever the circumstances. I know what it is to be in need, and I know what it is to have plenty. I have learned the secret of being content in any and every situation, whether well fed or hungry, whether living in plenty or in want" (Philippians 4:10–12).

Learning to be content with where God has placed you will relieve a lot of stress. You will have greater peace and happiness.

4. Trust

Trust is essential to good interpersonal relationships. You can't call someone a close friend if you don't trust him. You don't know if what he tells you is true. This creates doubt and uneasiness. Distrust destroys friendships.

Trust, on the other hand, builds up relationships. When you have a friend who has proven himself to be trustworthy, you confide in him and believe that what he tells you is true. That is a friendship worth having.

God is the most trustworthy person in the universe. He will never let you down. David reminds us, "Blessed is the man who makes the LORD his trust" (Psalm 40:4). Isaiah adds, "Surely God is my salvation; I will trust and not be afraid" (Isaiah 12:2). "Trust in the LORD with all your heart and lean not on your own understanding" (Proverbs 3:5).

Experiencing trust in your earthly relationships brings fulfillment and emotional health. Trust in Jesus brings peace, security, and salvation.

5. Courage

Courage opens the door for you to take on challenging new opportunities. God's people, ancient Israel, were at the Jordan River with Egypt behind them and Canaan in front of them. There was only one problem. Strong, warlike tribes occupied the land between them and Canaan, and these warriors were ready to defend their land. Moses challenged the children of Israel, "Be strong and courageous. Do not be afraid or terrified because of them, for the LORD your God goes with you; he will never leave you nor forsake you" (Deuteronomy 31:6). He told Joshua the same thing: "Be strong and courageous" (verse 7).

You may face some health challenges. You may be facing other life challenges. Face them with courage, not fear. God won't leave or forsake you. With God, you can face with courage every challenge that lies before you.

6. Joy

Joy is the "expression of keen pleasure."[5] It's the emotion of great delight or happiness based on the contentment that comes only from God. Everyone wants to experience joy. What about joy *all the time?* Is that possible? Jesus wants you to be joyful all the time, no matter what the circumstances of your life. "A merry heart does good, like medicine, / But a broken spirit dries the bones" (Proverbs 17:22, NKJV). Jesus said to His disciples, "I have told you this so that my joy may be in you and that your joy may be complete" (John 15:11). He has promised complete and total joy for His children.

How do we obtain joy? Jesus said, "Ask and you will receive, and your joy will be complete" (John 16:24). Not only can you have joy, but He promises that you can have complete joy. And this joy is the result of experiencing the indwelling power of the Holy Spirit in your life. "The fruit of the Spirit is . . . joy" (Galatians 5:22).

7. Peace

Nations at war cry out for peace. So does the human soul. Jesus said, "Peace I leave with you, My peace I give to you; not as the world gives do I give to you. Let not your heart be troubled, neither let it be afraid" (John 14:27, NKJV). With Jesus, we can all live in peace—with each other and with ourselves. We won't be troubled or fearful. Like joy, peace results from the indwelling of the Holy Spirit. "The fruit of the Spirit is. . . peace" (Galatians 5:22). Peace is a large part of emotional health.

8. Thanksgiving

America celebrates Thanksgiving one day a year. May I suggest making every day, every meal, one of thanksgiving? Paul tells us in Philippians 4:4 to "rejoice in the Lord always. I will say it again: Rejoice!" When you are rejoicing, you are thinking pleasant, positive thoughts. Rejoicing in God brings true, everlasting joy and happiness.

Would you like to have an evening full of joy and thanksgiving? Take a pen and a piece of paper. Make a list of the good things God has given to you. Start back as far as you can remember—back to your youth and childhood. You may even think of some things you thought were terrible at the time, but now, when you look back, you can see that God brought good out of them (see Romans 8:28). List those things too. When you have written down everything you can think of, bow your head and "offer unto God thanksgiving" (Psalm 50:14, KJV). The book of Hebrews tells us, "By Him [Jesus] let us continually offer the sacrifice of praise to God, that is, the fruit of our lips, giving thanks to His name" (Hebrews 13:15, NKJV).

You don't need to fear the future. God has told you He will take care of you, so you can face retirement with thanksgiving, courage, and hope. These years can be filled with joy, love, contentment, and peace. These fruits of the Spirit are God's gifts to you so that you can have a happy, healthy retirement.

HOMEWORK:

1. List the stressors that are affecting your life now.
2. Write down some practical ways you can reduce the stress in your life.
3. Ask yourself: "Whom do I need to forgive?" "What keeps me from forgiving that person/those people?" "Do I need to forgive myself for anything?" "Do I need to ask forgiveness of anyone and make things right?"
4. List at least ten things for which you are thankful.
5. List at least three things that give you hope.
6. List at least three things that give you joy.
7. List any anxieties or fears you need to give to God in order to find peace.

---

1. See Frank Minirth and Paul Meir, *Happiness Is a Choice* (Grand Rapids, Mich.: Baker Book House, 1994).

2. Don Hall makes these points in his "Coping With Stress" lecture, which is part of his Eight Weeks to Wellness seminar.

3. James A. Blumenthal et al, "Effects of Exercise Training on Older Patients With Depression," *Archives of Internal Medicine* 159, (October 25, 1999), 2349-2355.

4. Schneider and Miles, 148, 149.

5. *Webster's New Universal Unabridged Dictionary,* 1989.

CHAPTER 9

Social Health

Sometimes people touch our lives in ways that we don't even realize until they're gone. A friend of mine told me of just such a man—Gary Robinson. Here is the story as she told it to me:

Gary ran a shoeshine stand in the lobby of the Hilton hotel in Altamonte Springs, Florida. He was an unassuming Black man around sixty, with a stocky frame and an ever-present smile. He liked people, and people liked him. Gary couldn't let anyone pass without a pleasant word or smile. He seemed to know what each person needed to hear.

As a sales manager, I showed many people around the hotel. Gary was one of my selling points. I would walk through the lobby and point out the restaurant and the car rental counter and then I would say, "We even have a professional shoeshine man." Gary would chuckle at the word *professional* and then charm the guests without even trying. He had many repeat clients. Many times when I passed by, he would have one gentleman up on the chair shining his shoes while another waiting customer showed Gary pictures of his children and family.

When I came to work on Wednesday, May 3, 2004, I noticed that Gary was not sitting in his usual place. I thought that maybe he had a doctor's appointment. It wasn't until later in the day that the word spread that he had died of a heart attack the night before.

As people found out that Gary had died, a small memorial of cards and flowers appeared on his shoeshine stand. In the days and weeks following his death, I was amazed at the number of people who congregated beside his stand to share how he had touched their lives. The general manager of the Hilton called Gary an "ambassador" for the hotel.

Gary wasn't just shining shoes, he was shining people. Even people who never sat in his chair knew and remembered him. He was a bright spot to many weary travelers, and those whose lives he touched will greatly miss him. Gary was making a difference in his own way. Every community needs a Gary Robinson.

The importance of social connections

Research shows that one important factor for aging well is staying connected to people. It is important to stay involved with people from our church and our community. These connections not only are vital to social health but also affect the other kinds of health. Let's look at how staying healthy socially affects physical, emotional, and intellectual health.

1. Lower mortality risk

Did you know that having friends can help you live longer? A famous study done in Alameda County, California, followed a group of sixty-nine hundred people for nine years. Those who had close friends tended to live longer than those with poor social support systems. In fact, irrespective of age, the risk of death of those who had close relationship with others, whether friends or family members, was two to four times lower than that of those who had no significant relationships.[1]

2. Better emotional health

There is a close correlation between social connections and emotional health. The term used in social science is *psychosocial*. We were created to support and fulfill each other, not to live relying only on self. The strength of social contacts influences our emotional vitality, which encompasses feeling happy, enjoying life, feeling hopeful about the future, having a sense of self-acceptance, and having little to no anxiety or depression.[2]

3. Less cognitive decline

Social interaction plays a vital role in helping to maintain reasoning ability. In a study of 2,812 people over the age of sixty-five, researchers found that compared to people who had no social ties, those who had five or six good social ties were 2.4 times less likely to experience decline in their reasoning ability over the twelve years of follow-up.[3] What a difference good friends can make in our lives!

Some factors make obtaining social health more difficult. However, you can have social health no matter what your circumstances are. To improve your social health, evaluate your situation and do whatever you can to make positive changes in your life. It's like pedaling up a hill on a bicycle—as long as you're pedaling forward, you can't roll back downhill.

People may have different ideas about what makes life meaningful. Some people, because of their natural temperament, don't enjoy socializing as much as others do. That's OK. Evaluate where you are and where you want to be.

Major life changes may affect your social health. Aging often brings changing circumstances, such as retirement, relocation, health changes, and the death of friends. These can all be difficult events, but you can overcome them. Surround yourself with friends, both old and new, and allow them to help you with whatever you're facing. Some of them may have faced similar situations.

The friendship scale

The quality of your social ties is just as important as the quantity of friends you have. Some of your social contacts will be more casual, but you'll benefit from having at least one or two very meaningful relationships.

How can you determine whether or not you have enough good friends? Let's look at a continuum concept called the friendship scale.[4]

1	2	3	4	5	6	7	8	9	10
Acquaintances				Friends			Deep relationships		

Level 1 represents our most casual acquaintances. Level 10 signifies those with whom we have the deepest relationships—the most intimate relationships two people can have. We may automatically think of marriage, but that doesn't have to be the case. Several Bible stories illustrate this level of closeness: David and Jonathan, Ruth and Naomi, Paul and Timothy.

Five qualities stand out as essential to a level 10 relationship. The first is trust. David and Jonathan trusted each other completely. They spent time building up that trust. Trust is established through experiences in which both people show themselves to be trustworthy. Suppose a total stranger were to walk up to you on the street and ask for a thousand-dollar loan. Would you say Yes? I hope not. What if you received the same request from a very close friend? Your response would probably be different. Trust makes the difference—knowing you will get your money back.

The second ingredient important to a level 10 relationship is acceptance. As with trust, a level 10 relationship means total acceptance. Some friendships are limited because people find it difficult to accept someone with whom they disagree. You can accept people whether or not you agree with them. You needn't allow your differences to get in the way of the friendship.

The third quality is commitment. To have a level 10 relationship, you must be willing to commit yourself to that person, to that relationship. You can't say, "I really like you, but don't ask anything of me." That is not a level 10 relationship. Commitment means you're willing to do everything you can to have the closest relationship possible.

Fourth is responsibility. There is no way around it. I was driving home very late one night—2 A.M.—when my car broke down. I called my friend Wayne on my cell phone. "Wayne, I'm sorry to call you in the middle of the night, but I'm stranded." Before I could say any more, Wayne interrupted, "Where are you? . . . I'll be right there." That describes what a close friend will do. If Wayne were only a level 1 friend, he would have said, "Just call a tow truck," and hung up the phone.

Finally, a level 10 friendship requires mutual respect. That includes respecting your friend even when you know his or her weaknesses. Respect can create a bridge over many disagreements. When you respect someone, it means you are willing to listen to that person.

It is possible to have a friend who is a level 10 in most but not all of the five areas we just discussed. That's OK. No friendship is perfect. It takes work to maintain the friendship level you have and more work to increase the level. But it can be done if both of you are willing to spend the necessary time and effort.

In addition to family members, you can usually have only from two to four other individuals who are in levels 8 through 10. You only have so much time and emotional energy to maintain that level of relationship. On the other hand, you can have hundreds of acquaintances because acquaintanceship requires only low levels of commitment and responsibility. Jesus had twelve disciples. All were dear friends to Him, but of the twelve, three were extra-special: Peter, James, and John.

On the scale, consider levels 1, 2, and 3 to be acquaintances. Note how much lower the level of trust, acceptance, commitment, and responsibility are than they would be in a level 10 relationship. These are people all around you: neighbors, people at church, people you meet shopping. Some of them you know only because of their occupation, like your barber or beautician. You say you know them, yet you don't really know them. You relate to them on level 1.

Levels 4 through 7 comprise people whom you would consider friends. These are people whom you know better than acquaintances but who are not as close as those on levels 8 to 10. This middle group of friends is very important. They help make life meaningful. They're the people you call on the phone. They come to your house. You go to their houses. They're on your greeting card list for holidays and birthdays.

In retirement, you have more time for friends, and your retired friends have more time for you. Take advantage of that extra time. Friendships don't just happen; they take time and effort. If you invest in your friendships, they will stand the test of time.

Because getting older often involves changes such as retirement or relocation and even losing older friends to death, you may find it necessary to make new friends. If you want friends, you must be friendly. Be open and honest with people. Be willing to share and even take the risk of rejection. It's worth it!

Improve your social health

Let's say you have a terrific group of close friends. What else can you do to improve your social health? Remember Gary Robinson? He was always giving of his time and wisdom to make other people's lives better.

1. Volunteer

Volunteering is a great way to get out in the community, make new friends, and make a positive difference for other people. Many wonderful organizations need people to contribute their talents, time, and energies. Habitat for Humanity, the organization that former president Jimmy Carter works for, uses the skills of thousands of volunteers. Every hospital benefits tremendously from the resources of volunteers. Organizations that provide humanitarian aid to poverty-stricken countries need people for medical help and construction all over the world.

You may think you don't have anything to contribute. That couldn't be further from the truth. In the year 2000, an average of 5,574 people reached their sixty-fifth birthday every day. The day you reach your sixty-fifth birthday, you still have the wisdom, skills, and talents that you had the day before. Why not harness them to do something good for someone else? In fact, you don't have to wait until your sixty-fifth birthday to do this. Do something now.

To start the process, evaluate your talents and interests, and then look for an organization that fits you. Look in the yellow pages under "volunteer services" or "social service organizations." Perhaps you're already interested in a nearby hospital, school, church, or other community organization. The opportunities are limitless. Perhaps you should look even closer to home—you may be able to help your children, grandchildren, or your neighbors.

Don't forget the needs of those in your own age group. You can make a wonderful contribution by helping other older adults remain healthy and independent and enjoy a high quality of life. When seniors help each other maintain happiness and security, they make one of their greatest contributions to the community. Let's not simply live and let live. Rather, let's live and *help* live.

2. Mentor

You may also contribute to your community through mentoring. Consider the possibilities. You could mentor a child or young person. There are many Adopt-a-Grandchild-type programs already established. You could also contact your local school or church to find out about setting up your own program.

Another option is to mentor a young couple who are struggling through some tough times. A retired neighbor of ours helped a couple secure a home and worked with them on financial mentoring. What a fantastic opportunity for both families!

A third option is to mentor another senior. Though some may not consider this mentoring, it is just as valuable as the other types of mentoring. If you are computer savvy, mentor a senior who would like to learn how to email family and friends. If you play the piano, mentor another who would like to learn. Do you enjoy photography, painting, or needlework? You can probably find someone with whom to share your skills. Mentoring is an excellent way to pull your weight in society and make a significant contribution to another's quality of life.

3. Become an entrepreneur

Among the 5,574 people turning sixty-five every day are some highly motivated, energetic, visionary people. They desire to change things for the better, to make a difference in their community. In the world of business, entrepreneurs are people who see a need and do something to fill that need. Instead of asking, "Why doesn't someone do something?" they step up to the plate and say, "I'll make something happen." They have a dream, they create a plan, and they sell their idea to other interested persons. They start an organization, and things happen. Does that describe you?

Ray, a retired church financial and business executive, saw a financial need in a church-supported day academy. At seventy-three years of age, he said, "I want to use my business skills to help start a health-food store." He explored the idea with interested friends. After some organizational meetings and financial planning, Ray, along with a core group of supporters, started the store. Friends and community members volunteer their time. Students from the school work in the store. Not only does the community benefit from healthier food options, but financially challenged students earn some of their tuition as well. During a five-year stretch, the store added fifty thousand dollars to the school's budget. And the benefits are not all financial. The volunteers enjoy the feeling of making an important contribution to the community.

If you have business skills, you may want to take on the challenge of organizing a nonprofit organization. Such an organization might provide any of the following kinds of services:

- Senior companions—offering help with household tasks and care on a short- or long-term basis
- Financial counseling
- Family counseling
- Home repair and maintenance
- Weight-management for seniors
- Legal counseling
- Educational and entertainment traveling for seniors
- In-home meal preparation or a Meals on Wheels type of organization

4. Start an "I Belong" group

Even if you're not an entrepreneur, you can do many things to enhance your social health. In the interviews I conducted to determine what is important to older people, two themes kept arising: friendship and helping others. All of the outreach opportunities we have looked at so far combine both of these elements to a certain extent, but perhaps the best way of connecting these two goals is to form an "I Belong" group.

An "I Belong" group is a group of four to eight people who want to become very close friends. They form a close-knit group whose members promise to help each other in any way they can. Each member of the group knows he or she is an important part of the group. If one person has a need or a problem, all the other members pitch in to help that person.

The group may meet once or twice a week. They may have social activities, such as game nights, eating together, or attending concerts. They may also choose to do physical activities together, such as walking around the mall for exercise. They may study Scripture together. The sky is the limit. Discuss among yourselves what you want to do as a group.

The main purpose of the group is to support each other. If one member of the group becomes sick, others will make sure that person is cared for. If someone's car breaks down, group members can provide transportation. Each person in the group will experience a sense of belonging, of being loved. Caring for, nurturing, and supporting others in your group not only benefits those being helped but also helps you stay engaged in life and remain socially healthy.

"One another" texts

How can we develop close friendships? Dale Carnegie's book *How to Win Friends and Influence People* is a classic on the subject. It has sold more than eight million copies. However, centuries before Dale Carnegie, the Bible gave us seven classic principles of how we can develop close friendships. The New Testament ties all these principles to the Greek word *allēlōn,* which is translated in the English Bible as "one another." This word is always paired with another word, such as *pray* or *love:* "Pray one for another"; "love one another." Let's look at the *allēlōn* texts.

1. Love one another

Love is the foundation of friendship. The word *love* appears in the New Testament hundreds of times. Peter is one of the many writers who exhorted his readers to love each other. Near the beginning of one of his books, Peter wrote, "Love one another deeply, from the heart" (1 Peter 1:22). Later in the same book, he wrote, "Above all, love each other deeply, because love covers over a multitude of sins" (4:8). Clearly, love is something Peter believed was important for the believers to whom he wrote. It's a message that is still relevant for us today.

Do you believe we should love each other? If so, how do you put your beliefs into practice? You may have heard this before: "Don't just tell me about love. Show me that you love me." When we put love into action, we become willing to focus on finding solutions to whatever problems trouble our relationships. We become willing to forgive. Love makes individual differences bearable. "Hatred stirs up dissension, but love covers over all wrongs" (Proverbs 10:12).

Jesus calls love a commandment: "A new commandment I give you: Love one another. As I have loved you, so you must love one another. By this all men will know that you are my disciples, if you love one another" (John 13:34, 35). How will people know we are true followers of Christ? If we love each other. Followers of Jesus treat people with love. Jesus wants to pour His love through you, but He can do that only if you are receptive.

First Corinthians 13:4-8 tells us some characteristics of love: It is patient, kind, is not proud, keeps no record of wrongs, always protects, always trusts, always hopes, always perseveres. Is your love like that? If not, let Jesus fill you with His love. He loves you with never-ending love. He can't wait to shower it down on you. When you experience it, your natural response will be to share it with others.

2. Accept one another

"Accept one another . . . just as Christ accepted you, in order to bring praise to God" (Rom. 15:7). What does it mean to accept someone? Paul gives us a very clear example in Romans. We are to accept each other just as Christ accepted us. And how did Christ accept us? "While we were still sinners, Christ died for us" (Romans 5:8). To be a true friend to someone, accept that person just as she is, without expecting her to change. Don't reject that person just because she doesn't live up to your expectations. Jesus didn't say, "When you get all your kinks worked out, I'll accept you." He accepts you where you are right now, today. Then He lovingly asks you to invite Him in to work on the kinks.

When you first meet someone, you get acquainted with that person by asking questions. You learn where she's from, what she enjoys, and you learn about her family. You may find you have some things in common. If so, this leads to enjoyable conversation and activity. Finding that you have little in common can create an attitude of nonacceptance; you may not feel comfortable in her presence. How can you accept a person who is so different from you? Remember, different doesn't mean bad. Actually, meeting someone who differs from you provides an opportunity to gain new insights and to broaden your understanding, knowledge, and judgment.

True acceptance means accepting not only what you share in common with someone but also the differences. In fact, if all of your friends were just like you, life would be boring. An old saying reminds us that "variety is the spice of life." It's easy to gravitate to people who are like you. Why not specifically look for people who differ from you?

There's another old saying: "Opposites attract." If that holds true for you, then your spouse may be quite different from you. He may enjoy different things. Her idea of retirement may differ from yours. Accept one another. Many divorces can trace their start to nonacceptance. When you are more accepting of your spouse, you will have a more intimate relationship.

If you can't accept someone, you will build animosity, not friendship. Don't give up when you find that you are having difficulty accepting someone. There is hope. Acceptance is a process. God can change your attitude about someone if you ask Him to.

3. Pray for one another

The Bible says, "Pray for each other" (James 5:17). If love is the foundation of friendship, prayer is the glue that holds it together. Personal prayer helps not only your own spiritual growth and fellowship with God but also the person you are praying for.

Prayer is one of the most powerful bonding ties a person can experience. When a person prays for you, you know that person really cares for you. You feel loved and valued. You want to know that person better and build a closer friendship.

James 5:16 promises that the prayer of a righteous person is powerful and effective. Everyone needs prayer. Your friends need prayer every bit as much as you do. Who better to pray for them than you?

There is another aspect of praying for others. When we're praying for someone else, we're not looking for flaws. We can't hold a grudge against them. We're trying to protect them, not hurt them. Prayer draws us closer to the person we're praying for. It enhances friendship. It can also turn our enemies into friends. We cannot hate someone we're praying for.

4. Honor one another

Paul counseled, "Honor one another above yourselves" (Romans 12:10). To honor means to hold in high esteem, to respect. Not only are we to accept each other, we are to honor, to hold in high esteem and respect, those we consider friends. Do you have a favorite Christmas tree ornament? When you find it, where do you hang it? Most likely at the front and center of the tree. You place it in the most prominent place. This is how we are to treat people. Give them the place of honor. Honor your spouse, honor your children, honor your friends.

To honor someone is to make that person look good, rather than trying to direct people's attention to ourselves. When Itzhak Perlman plays a concerto with the New York Philharmonic, the orchestra accompanies him. The other musicians help Perlman to make the best of the piece of music. They honor him by playing their parts softly so the audience can hear him. When you honor someone, you allow that person to be heard, even if it means you can't say what you want to say.

5. Encourage one another

"Encourage one another" (1 Thessalonians 5:11). The world is full of problems. Each of us faces our own personal struggles. When one of your friends is facing challenges, your encouragement brings welcome relief. "You can do it!" are wonderful words to those who are filled with doubt.

6. Carry one another's burdens

"Carry each other's burdens" (Galatians 6:2). Verbal encouragement is good, but action is even better. Carrying a friend's burden is action. All the stages of life bring difficult situations. As we already mentioned, stress is a major burden that people carry. What action can you take to help relieve your friends' stress?

Joyce Pifer, a seventy-four-year-old retired nurse, saw a need. Many in her community had health needs that traditional healthcare agencies were not adequately meeting. Joyce used her nursing and administrative skills to organize a parish nursing program at the Walker Memorial Adventist Church in Avon Park, Florida. She built the parish nurse program to its current size of eleven volunteer registered nurses along with six helpers.

When someone is discharged from the hospital or is just ill or disabled, a volunteer nurse from Joyce's agency goes into the home to find out what that person needs, such as food, meal preparation, respite care, or transportation to the doctor. The nurse evaluates various safety issues and tells the patient about services available in the community. Then the nurse assigns volunteers from the church to bring meals or to provide transportation to physician's appointments and perhaps even organizes some respite care for the caregivers. Most importantly, the nurse supports each member of the family through prayer, caring conversation, and love in action. This is carrying one another's burdens.

7. Serve one another

"Serve one another in love" (Galatians 5:13). We don't usually consider the activities connected with the word *serve* enjoyable. This word may even have a distasteful connotation. We may want to "help" someone, but to "serve" takes our willingness a step further. We're used to being served, not serving. Yet Jesus, God incarnate, became a servant. He served His disciples by washing their dusty feet (see John 13:1-17). He concluded this act of service by saying, "I have set you an example that you should do as I have done for you" (verse 15). Jesus wants you to follow His lead and serve your fellow human beings.

"How can I serve?" you might ask. Service is far more than just doing something for someone else. If you help someone merely out of a sense of duty, your body language will make that clear. That is not true service. Only when you can totally forget self and think only of that other person and what he or she needs will you be serving as Christ served.

No one is an island. What you do affects other people. If you can unselfishly serve those around you, not only will you have deeper, more meaningful friendships, but the world will also be a better place.

The retirement years are prime-time years for enjoying life. Friends are important. Social health is more than just being engaged with friends and involved in your community. To enjoy prime-time living is to make a difference in your community and on your block. It means helping others enjoy life a little more. Take the concepts of this chapter to heart. Maybe you will be inspired to do volunteer work or start an "I Belong" group. Whatever God leads you to do, ask Him to make you a Gary Robinson in your community.

HOMEWORK:

1. Think of the people you know, and rate your relationship with them on the friendship scale. Are there some friendships you would like to develop more deeply?
2. Write down some of the things you want to do in your community to give back some of the talents God gave you.
3. What do you want to do to connect to others socially?

1. John W. Rowe and Robert L. Kahn, *Successful Aging* (New York: Pantheon Books, 1998), 241, 242.

2. Miller, 150

3. Ball and Birge, 495.

4. I first saw this scale in a book by Bruce Fisher.

CHAPTER

Developing a Prime-Time Aging Strategy

You have now reached the most important part of this book. This is the most exciting and critical time. If you've been doing the homework with each chapter, you've actually already started your plan for prime-time aging. You're already on your way to optimal health and quality of life, whatever your stage of life now. You'll have the energy to do the things you've always dreamed of doing during your retirement years.

The concepts in this book can help you only if you're committed to making changes in your life. Change is not easy, but if you stick to it, your strategy will pay off. The goals in your prime-time aging strategy will, of course, vary with your age. But don't think that you're too young or too old to begin. No matter what your age, right now is the time to start investing in your future. The younger you are, the more impact your strategy can have. You would earn more dividends for your retirement on ten thousand dollars invested at age twenty-six than at age sixty-four. Likewise, the younger you are when you begin prime-time living, the more time you have to enjoy its benefits.

For those of you who are sixty-five or older, developing your prime-time aging strategy right now is important for another reason. Let's compare life to a football game. It's the fourth quarter with only two minutes remaining in the game. Your team is behind by four points. You have the football on your opponent's fifteen-yard line, and you must score a touchdown to win the game. At this point in the game, every play becomes more important, not less important. In life, you may be just beginning the "last quarter" of your game. It's crucial that you have a good game plan and make the right plays to maximize your chances of "winning"—making every year of life happy, healthy, and vibrant.

Some of you are just starting the second half of your game, but you may already be a little behind. For example, you may be a little overweight and out of shape. Your cholesterol level may be higher than it should be. It is not too late to get serious and make a game plan that guarantees your success. Remember, in terms of your health, good "plays" will not only score points now but also help you win in the end.

Let's get started in developing a prime-time aging strategy. We'll do it in seven steps. We'll start with some basic guidelines, and then explain each of the steps.

Basic guidelines

It's essential that you keep your strategy simple. If it becomes too complex, you may not complete it. Start small, and set yourself a reasonable time line rather than trying to accomplish too many things at once.

Focus on the end result. Describe what you want your retirement to look like, and then determine the steps you'll need to take to reach your goal. Think of each day as an opportunity to get closer to your goals.

Make your plan fun. Avoid living with the burden of a bunch of rules. If one of your goals is to exercise more, find an activity you enjoy rather than something that will be a chore. If it's fun, you'll be more likely to continue doing it.

You may have twenty to thirty—or even more—years of retirement. You can accomplish quite a few things in that time. However, you should start your plans small so that you don't get overwhelmed. Think about today, tomorrow, and this week before you think about planning the next twenty years in minute detail.

If your spouse has also developed a strategy, try to blend both strategies together so you each benefit from the other's vision. Don't allow one strategy to become more important than the other. Working with your spouse to accomplish your goals will strengthen your relationship.

It's time to get started. All of the seven steps are important to a successful strategy, so don't skip anything. To give you ideas and help you think about your own plan, each step contains suggestions from strategies other people have developed. At the end of this chapter, you'll have a chance to go through the seven steps yourself.

Step 1: Write your mission statement

Your personal mission statement is your reason for living. It may be something like this: "I want to share myself in a personal relationship with God, family, friends, and neighbors, while being active in the community and church." Another example is: "I want to glorify God through all areas of my life by listening to the Holy Spirit and having meaningful relationships with the people God has brought into my life." Though slightly different, both these mission statements give purpose to the people who wrote them. God uses your understanding about the purpose for your life to bring you happiness. Your mission statement will strongly influence the rest of your prime-time aging strategy.

When you write your mission statement, decide what purpose you want your life to serve. Think about what makes you experience fulfillment and happiness. Your mission statement may be similar to those mentioned above or it may be entirely different. It may even change slightly as you get older. The most important thing is that you think carefully about why you are here—your *raison d'être,* or reason for being.

You may have seen the bumper sticker that reads, "I'm spending my children's inheritance." People may say that simply to get a laugh or two, but some actually live that way. Their mission statement might read: "Eat, drink, and be merry, for tomorrow we die." I hope this isn't your philosophy.

As you go through life, your purpose influences how you live. Whether or not you've thought about it, something motivates your decisions and reactions. Now you have a chance to explore and expand your mission statement so that it can help you prioritize what you want in life, both now and in the future.

Step 2: Identify who you are

The question "Who am I?" is difficult to answer. Too often we equate who we are with what we do. If that's the only way you define yourself, you'll be in trouble when you retire. Who we are and what we do are in fact quite different.

I pastored churches for nineteen years but I'm no longer employed as a pastor. I have many different answers to the question of my identity: "I am God's son. I am a husband, a father, a grandfather. I am a son. I am a brother. I am a friend. I am a neighbor. I am part of my community and a member of my church." All of those answers work together to make me who I am. They are important relationships that make up my identity. Who are you?

In addition to the roles you have, the characteristics that make up your personality also answer the question "Who am I?" For instance, I consider myself to be energetic, outgoing, and on the go much of the time. You may want to look at your own characteristics, for this will undoubtedly determine how and why you enjoy doing certain things and will help determine your goals. The way you see yourself, both inside and outside, is very important. Evaluating this will help you design your personal prime-time aging strategy.

Step 3: Write down your personal health history

What is your personal health history? This includes more than just your medical history. It includes also the other five areas of health—financial, intellectual, emotional, social, and spiritual. Was there a time in your life when your spiritual or emotional health was not what it should have been? Have you had some traumatic events in your life that you haven't dealt with? Health history is such a broad area that you should focus on things that will influence decisions still to be made.

Most likely, your health history isn't perfect. It is the work of a lifetime and will be a work in progress as long as you live. When reviewing your health history, don't be too hard on yourself. You can't change the past. The good news is that God is in the business of loving and caring for you no matter what. He wants you to enjoy a healthy life (see John 10:10; 3 John 2).

1. Physical health

I'm sixty-five, but I still remember a decision I made early in life that has been a health benefit ever since. It occurred on my family's farm outside Charlotte, North Carolina. One Sunday when I was about ten years of age, fried chicken was served for dinner. I announced, "I don't want any chicken." My cousin Carl, who was visiting that day, says he still remembers that meal. He recalls me saying, "Poor little chicken; poor little chicken." The day before, that chicken had been one of my pets. Now it was dinner.

My decision extended even further. In addition to not eating chicken, I decided not to eat the cow I had milked. That cow had been butchered and put into the freezer. My decision to become a vegetarian was not based on how much saturated fat and cholesterol was in the steak or how high my cholesterol was. It was based on a ten-year-old boy's love for his pet calves and chickens. I believe that the decision has served me well, for both my physical and my emotional health.

I made my next pivotal health decision many years later. I had just finished college and moved to Chesapeake, Virginia. Another young man who attended the same church asked me to go running, and I accepted the invitation. Up to that time, I had never run for exercise because I had gotten all the exercise I needed doing farm chores. However, at this point in his life, I was selling Bible storybooks door to door—a very stressful job. I didn't realize at that time how important that decision to start running would be. It helped reduce my stress level and kept my weight under control, as well as providing some social time with my friend Bruce. Most importantly, it started me out on what is one of my best health habits. Running and walking are essential components of my prime-time aging strategy, in addition to swimming and bicycling.

Ten years after I started running with Bruce, I was attending seminary, working on my doctor of ministry degree. One of the classes I took became life changing: Ministry of Healing, taught by Harold Habenicht, M.D. Dr. Habenicht taught principles from Scripture and the book *The Ministry of Healing.* Those principles expanded my thinking, becoming an integral part of my life—and, though I didn't realize it at the time, part of my prime-time aging strategy. One of the class requirements was to run a mile and a half. At the time, I was thirty-four years old and competing against students in their twenties. The goal was to complete the run in twelve minutes. Yes, I made it!

Fast-forward approximately thirteen years. While living in New Jersey, I faced what was to be my most challenging health issue yet—my weight. This problem came as a real surprise to me because I'd always been thin. At the beginning of my junior year of high school, I was five feet ten inches tall and weighed one hundred pounds. At forty-two, I weighed 155 pounds. At that point I had decided I wanted to lose five pounds—and I did it relatively easily, by running four or five times a week for a couple weeks.

But five years later, my weight had crept up to 191 pounds. That was a real problem! I decided I only had two options: either change the picture I had of myself as being thin and create a new picture of myself as overweight, or lose thirty pounds. I chose the latter option. I didn't use pills or strange fad diets, just regular exercise and a healthier diet that eliminated some of the less healthy foods and snacks between meals. It was a great choice! Although it took seven months, I reached my goal and felt good about it. Now, maintaining a healthy weight is an enduring part of my prime-time aging strategy.

2. Financial health

Another aspect of your health history comprises your financial decisions—how they are affecting you now, and how they will affect you later. If you've made poor decisions in the past, you can learn from those mistakes and make different decisions for the future.

Have a financial planner help you develop some goals and the plans to achieve those goals during a reasonable time. You may want to think about investing in some real estate or starting a Roth IRA. Try to set aside 10 percent of your salary in a retirement fund. Continuing that habit will allow you to have greater peace of mind in the future.

3. Spiritual health

This is perhaps the most difficult part of life to measure. You can't step on a scale to determine whether or not you are spiritually underweight. One of the most important decisions you can make is to spend time praying and listening to God every day. There are days when you may forget or allow other things to fill your devotional time. But when you spend that time with God in the morning, the rest of the day goes so much more smoothly.

As you evaluate your spiritual health history, think about how God has led you in the past. Sometimes God's voice was clearest during the most difficult times. One way to see how God has led you is to keep a prayer journal. Each day, write down your prayers and what God is saying to you through Scripture. Record the answers to your prayers and say "Thank You." When you are discouraged, you can look back at how God has led and realize that He is still working even though you might not be able to see it.

4. A total health-history evaluation

Take a look at the level of your health throughout your life in all the six areas. Don't disparage yourself or become discouraged because of your mistakes. God takes you where you are. He loves you and will never give up on you. He says, "I will never leave you or forsake you" (Deuteronomy 31:6).

Reviewing your health choices and actions may at times depress you. However, there are three important facts you can tell yourself as you proceed: (1) God has been interested in your life and will give you insights about health as you ask Him for guidance. (2) You have messed up at times, maybe through weight gain, poor diet, or lack of exercise—and we won't even talk about stress! But that is OK. Now is the time to learn from your mistakes and commit yourself to positive changes for the future. (3) Prime-time aging offers you a wonderful opportunity to gear up for retirement by improving the quality of your life.

Step 4: Determine what you enjoy and what you want to accomplish

You have examined your philosophy of life and written a mission statement. You have listed your roles and some of your personality traits. You have looked at your health history. Now it's time to begin getting your plans for the future down on paper. It's time to decide what you want to do with the rest of your life. You can limit this step to a few basic goals, or you can expand it to include numerous, detailed goals that you want to reach and enjoy in each of the six areas of health.

For instance, in the area of physical health, I have three goals that I want to achieve. The first is to feel good. The second is to avoid disease as long as possible. And my third goal is to maintain my physical strength and muscle tone as long as possible.

In the area of intellectual health, one of my goals is to learn how to use computers effectively. I want to learn to do research on the Internet. I want to learn to do seminar presentations using PowerPoint. I also want to be able to communicate using email. These are things I should have learned a long time ago but have neglected to focus on.

Sally, age sixty, has some very specific goals in the social and spiritual areas. She says, "People are very important to me. I have always been a little shy, so it's difficult for me to develop new friendships. One of my goals in the social area is to try to meet new people and spend time getting to know them."

Her spiritual goals are also very important to her. When I asked her what was most important to her life spiritually, she said, "One of my spiritual goals also involves people. Part of my mission statement is to 'have meaningful relationships with the people God has brought into my life.' I want God to be able to use me to speak to people. That requires continual listening and communion with God."

Step 5: Identify where you are now

This step involves evaluating where you are in each of the six areas compared to where you want to be. For example, if you want to be ready financially for retirement, look at what you are doing now to achieve that goal. It may be that you are doing enough, or you might not have started planning at all. To get where you want to go, you have to be honest with yourself about where you are right now.

Step 6: Figure out how to get where you want to be—the process

This step requires a long, hard look at your goals. Maybe your goal is to avoid disease. You may have a long road of preventive measures ahead of you, but if you accomplish your goal, the dividends will be great! You will have not only a better quality of life but also a longer life. God said, "If you diligently heed the voice of the LORD your God, . . . I will put none of the diseases on you which I have brought on the Egyptians" (Exodus 15:26, NKJV). If you follow God's blueprint for a healthy lifestyle, you can to a large degree avoid disease as you age. Remember that healthy aging is 65 to 70 percent lifestyle and only 30 to 35 percent genetics and other factors.

Whatever your goal, make a list of the things you can do to help you reach that objective. If you have a general physical health goal of avoiding disease, you might consider the following list:
- Exercise at least thirty minutes, six days a week.
- Eat a healthy diet that includes five to nine servings of fruits and vegetables every day; avoid trans-fats, keeping saturated fat intake low, eat unrefined grains (whole wheat, not white), and eat good fats, including nuts.
- Obtain the amount of sleep that I need. (Remember that this varies for different people.)
- Effectively manage the stress that comes into my life.
- Drink six to eight glasses of water every day.
- Keep up to date with the latest health research.

- Maintain balance in all aspects of my life and live temperately.
- Focus on my spiritual growth.
- Stay engaged in life socially.

Step 7: Prioritize—and get started

If the task looks overwhelming, remember Philippians 4:13, "I can do all things through Christ who strengthens me" (NKJV). You are never alone; you don't have to do it by yourself. God is there to help. Take it one step at a time.

Now it's time for you to begin. Grab that pen and paper and begin writing. Use the chart at the end of this chapter to help you, though you may want to use a separate sheet of paper so that you'll have more room. Start by writing out your mission statement, and then answer the question, "Who am I?" This will give you a mini picture of yourself. Next, pick an area you feel comfortable with and continue filling in the chart until you have completed each section. Choose something you want to accomplish or change about your life from one of your goals in Step 4. Then decide how you will accomplish that goal. If you need some ideas, have a friend help you brainstorm. Start with something that you will really enjoy. It should be something that will give you quick dividends. Your reward will be worth the effort. You can do it!

PRIME-TIME AGING STRATEGY WORKSHEET

(You may want to use a separate sheet of paper for each of the six different areas.)

Mission Statement:

_____

_____

Who am I?

_____

_____

Developing a Prime-Time Aging Strategy

	Physical	Financial	Intellectual	Emotional	Social	Spiritual
History (where I've been)						
What I want to enjoy and accomplish						
Where I am now						
How I'm going to get where I want to be						
My priorities— getting started						

CHAPTER 11

Death and Dying

Think back to the first time you encountered the death of someone you knew and loved. Although you now know that death is an inevitable part of life, the first time you saw it must have been a shocking experience. Since you first grappled with death, you've probably experienced many other losses: beloved pets, grandmothers, aunts, uncles, classmates, friends, parents, and perhaps even a spouse. Death is one of life's greatest and most inevitable challenges. In addition to grief for the loss of someone you care about, it also brings you face to face with your own mortality.

Clive is ninety-one years of age. He was a missionary for many years and worked in his church's world office. He and Ellen were married for fifty-two years when tragedy struck. She was diagnosed with a terminal illness and died shortly thereafter. Clive was devastated. However, one of his longtime friends helped him through the grieving process, and after several years, Clive married her. Less than a year later, she suffered a massive stroke and was moved to a nursing home. For three years Clive visited her every day, and then she also died.

After much grieving, Clive felt he was finally able to move on. He met a lovely retired university professor, Janice. After seven years of marriage, tragedy struck again. Janice was diagnosed with Alzheimer's disease. When asked how he maintains his spirit, Clive replies, "[Taking care of Janice] is my work; there are more ups than downs." In other words, Clive sees his ministry as caring for those in his life no matter what difficult circumstances may arise. Some individuals suffer more losses than others do. In spite of all the losses Clive has had to face, he maintains a happy and positive spirit. He rates his happiness as an eight on a ten-point scale. What a positive attitude!

No one goes far in life without experiencing some kind of loss. The older you get, the more frequently these losses occur. And they bring deep pain. When I worked as a hospital chaplain, I had the difficult job of informing families when their loved ones died. The responses ranged from sobbing, to shrieks of terror, to angry kicking of the walls. There are no words that can remove the pain of seeing a loved one die or the horror people feel when they receive a phone call in the middle of the night informing them of a death. We cannot ever prepare ourselves for this extreme loss. So, the question looms: How should we handle the pain of losing a loved one to death?

David, the psalmist, may have given the best answer to that question when he wrote, "Yea, though I walk through the valley of the shadow of death, I will fear no evil: for thou art with me" (Psalm 23:4, KJV). Dealing with the pain of death is a process. It is like going through a deep, dark valley. The bad news is that we must go through the valley of pain, of grieving the loss. No one can go through that valley for us. The good news is that we don't simply go into the valley, we go through it. And the best news is that God is always with us. Through Isaiah, God has promised, "Fear thou not, I will strengthen thee. . . . I will help thee; . . . yea I will uphold thee" (Isaiah 41:10, KJV). God can bring healing when we face the pain of grief.

Grief recovery

Grieving is a complicated process. Whether we're grieving for a loved one or because we learn that our own death is imminent, grieving comes in different stages. In her book *On Death and Dying*,[1] Elisabeth Kubler-Ross discusses five common stages of grieving people pass through when they learn they will soon die. Many grief specialists have also successfully applied these stages to grieving for the death of a loved one. This is only a sketch; the process may vary widely for different people. The stages do not necessarily proceed in order. People may even skip one of them. And different people take differing amounts of time to go through the stages. Some even say that this is only the beginning of the grieving process.

The grieving process initiated at the death of a spouse often lasts years. The most important things we can do are to allow our emotions to come out and then to find closure for our pain through whatever avenues are right for us. Later in this chapter we will look at the acronym TEAR, which grief counselors often use to help with grief resolution. First, let's look at Kubler-Ross's five stages of grief: denial, anger, bargaining, depression, and acceptance.

1. Shock/denial

First, people experience shock and denial, even stubborn disbelief. Thoughts like "this can't be happening to me" flood the mind. They may have feelings of numbness and indecision. A woman whose sister had just died screamed, "Don't tell me!" She felt that if she didn't hear the words, it wouldn't be real. Shock and denial are God's anesthetic to deep emotional pain. Just as physical shock cushions physical pain, so emotional shock cushions emotional pain. In a sense, it eases people into acknowledging that they have suffered a loss.

While people's brains are telling them that the loss is raw reality, their emotions are saying, *I don't want to accept this.* Because the pain is so intense, many people experience apathy toward everything, even living itself. This is part of the healing process. It helps to share one's feelings with family and friends. And Christians have Someone else on their side. God the Father knows the pain of a Son's death. He helps His people through this very painful experience.

2. Anger

The second stage of grieving is anger. The feelings of anger may be manifested in very different ways, depending on the nature of the loss. A woman whose husband dies may be angry with

God for allowing it to happen. A mother whose son is killed in a street drag race will be angry, but she may have a difficult time expressing that anger—especially if the other driver was her son's best friend. She'll be angry with both boys for doing such a stupid thing and causing her so much pain, though she'll find it easier to express her anger toward her son's friend than to admit she's angry with her son. A widow may cry out, "Why did you [her husband] leave me when I needed you?" or "Why didn't you take better care of yourself? Why didn't you listen to the doctor?" A widower may yell, "Where were you, God, when my wife was killed? Don't you know how much she loved you? She served you all her life!"

People may direct their anger at God, at the person who died, at the doctor, or at whomever else they can blame for causing the loss, whether or not the connection is rational. Anger expresses how people feel about their loss. It is real, and it is good. Expressing anger is part of the healing process. People who are angry shouldn't deny their feelings. If they do, they may become stuck in one of the stages of grieving and never finish the process. This can cause serious emotional damage.

Dorothy lost her husband to a heart attack when he was only fifty-nine years old. She refused to deal with her loss. Her grieving process stopped at the second stage. Anger became the predominant theme in her life. Friends and family members did what they could to help her, but it was never enough. Dorothy's daughter Sandy said she could no longer let her mother stay with her because it was too emotionally destructive. Dorothy lost her emotional health because she didn't grieve adequately.

Anger can be destructive if people express it through violence or acts of revenge. It is good only when it helps motivate people to find a way to resolve their pain. John Walsh, the star of *America's Most Wanted,* found a way to use his anger beneficially. When his young son was savagely murdered, John was irate. His anger motivated him to develop the idea for *America's Most Wanted,* a TV show that helps find criminals and bring them to justice. As a result, thousands of criminals have been apprehended with the help of concerned viewers.

3. Bargaining

Bargaining is the third part of the process of healing grief. It can take many forms. A husband whose wife has a terminal disease may bargain: "God, if You'll heal my wife, I'll serve You more faithfully." A widow may bargain, "Just let me die too." Terminal patients ask to live until "my first grandchild is born in four months," or "until Christmas," or until some other event important to them. The Bible includes an example: Hezekiah, king of Judah, bargained for added years of life.

While bargaining is an important part of the grieving process, it can present challenges. Combined with the emotional stress brought on by the death, it may impede good decision-making. Susan's story stands as a warning, though the loss she was grieving came through divorce rather than death.

Together, Susan and Steve, her husband, owned a large farm. Then Steve left Susan for another woman. He wanted to farm the whole property, but he couldn't afford to buy Susan's half. Against the advice of her attorney, Susan gave her half of the farm to Steve. She saw Steve's interest in the farm as an opportunity to regain his love. She thought her generosity would reveal her deep love and devotion to him and bring him back to her. However, Steve married the other woman and moved her to the farm.

Susan's half interest in the farm was her only bargaining asset, but because of her emotional crisis, she made an unwise decision. People need to remember that experiencing a loss may bring out the impulse to bargain. Those who are devastated by a loss need to ask for and listen to quality counsel. This may help them avoid costly mistakes.

4. Depression*

Depression is a state in which feelings of hopelessness and helplessness can seem overwhelming. Emotionally painful as it is, it plays an important role in the grieving cycle. For those who have lost a friend or neighbor through death, healing usually takes a

---

*The thoughts expressed in this section relate only to depression caused by a loss. If you have feelings that make you think of hurting yourself or someone else, please call a physician, counselor, or hospital.

relatively short time. The loss of a spouse, however, through either death or divorce, involves a much longer grieving process. A widow or widower may feel depressed for months or even years. Here are four steps that can help you if you're struggling with depression that is related to grieving. (For further help, read the section on depression in chapter 8 of this book.)

1. Seek God's help. When we're depressed, we should talk to God about our feelings. We can be honest with God. We can record in a prayer journal our loneliness and anger, our fears and anxieties. Reading the Psalms is also helpful. These songs are full of grieving and of God's saving response to that grief. God understands our pain. He can empathize with us because His Son, Jesus, was murdered. He'll give us peace and comfort. "Peace I leave with you; my peace I give you. I do not give to you as the world gives. Do not let your hearts be troubled and do not be afraid" (John 14:27).

2. Allow yourself to experience the pain. Human nature wants to escape pain—to take a pill, to run, to do anything except experience pain. That's a common reaction. To heal from grief, we must be willing to stop, sit down, and think about our loss—the death of someone we loved. It is OK for us to cry. We can just let the tears flow. We can talk about that person to the other family members. Doing so may create more tears. That's all right. Crying is actually healthy.

A grandmother was attending a grief recovery seminar because her husband had passed away. She shared how her daughter had forbidden her grandson to ask any questions about Grandpa. The daughter told the grandson, "Talking about Grandpa would make Grandma sad, and she would cry." In reality, Grandma really wanted and needed to talk about Grandpa, even though doing so might make her cry. Talking about him and grieving her loss would have helped bring healing to her. She needed to think, talk, and cry about Grandpa's death.

Talking to someone can facilitate healing. Keeping a journal can also help. Writing down our thoughts and feelings helps us pinpoint exactly what we're feeling and why—something very helpful in the healing process.

3. Take good care of your physical health. During a time of grief, we need to make sure we eat healthy, nutritious foods. Even though we may not feel like preparing or even eating the food, eating well while avoiding overeating will help us stay healthy physically so we can concentrate on emotional healing. It is also important that we exercise daily and obtain adequate sleep.

4. Reinvest in life. There comes a time when we must face life without our missing loved one. This is especially difficult if we've lost a spouse. Life will not be the same. However, though life is different, it doesn't have to be bad. We must find new ways to celebrate the times that were so special in the past. We must reach out to old friends and make new friends. We must create new memories, new experiences, and new traditions.

5. Acceptance

It is important that we live in the present. Acceptance of the loss of a loved one doesn't mean letting go of the past, but it does mean refusing to stay there. We have to accept the fact that things have changed. Facing life without someone we love is difficult, but life is waiting. Reaching the stage of acceptance doesn't mean we don't think about the past. It doesn't mean we don't miss our deceased loved one anymore. It is simply a decision to move on with life, forgetting the pain and keeping the memories.

We're making progress when we come to the point where we're "forgetting those things which are behind and reaching forward" (Philippians 3:13, NKJV). Paul didn't actually forget his past, good or bad, but he refused to live in it. He was living in the present. Acceptance means that we don't allow the past to control our decisions or dictate our current response to life. The past is a major part of who we are, but we must live in the present.

Grief professionals often use the concept of "grief work" to help the bereaved through grief resolution. The acronym TEAR summarizes one common definition of grief work:

T = To accept the reality of the loss
E = Experience the pain of the loss
A = Adjust to the new environment without the lost object
R = Reinvest in the new reality

This is grief work. It often occurs when everything is supposed to be back to normal—when friends have stopped calling, the court case is resolved, and everyone thinks the bereaved should be over it. It's at this point that real grieving begins. That's when we have to hang in there, to learn to depend on God.

Facing our own death

None of us wants to die. King Hezekiah of ancient Judah didn't want to die. He proved he was one of the few good kings of Judah when he led out in major spiritual and moral reforms within the nation. Judah hadn't had a king like Hezekiah since the days of kings David and Solomon. One day Hezekiah was stricken with a fatal disease. God sent a message to him through the prophet Isaiah: "Put your house in order, because you are going to die" (Isaiah 38:1). It's bad enough when a doctor says, "I don't think you are going to make it." But when a prophet brings that message from God . . .

It was too much for Hezekiah. He wept bitterly and bargained with God for more years of life. "Why, God? I've been a good king. I've done my best." God heard his prayer and granted him an extra fifteen years of life. I can almost hear him say, "Thank You, God!" Unfortunately, the rest of the story is not so pleasant. Those fifteen years were not his best years—nor Judah's. Both would have been better off without them. The wise man Solomon reminds us there is "a time to be born and a time to die" (Ecclesiastes 3:2). Let's leave to God when that time should be.

In contrast, think of the story of Moses. He was eighty years old and was out in the wilderness tending sheep when God said, "Moses, I have a work for you to do. I want you to lead My people out of Egypt to Canaan, the Promised Land." For the next forty years, Moses led Israel. He talked with God on Mount Sinai. He received the tablets of stone with the Ten Commandments carved in God's own handwriting. He directed the building of the sanctuary. He was one of the greatest men who ever lived—a spiritual and intellectual giant. Deuteronomy 34:10 tells us, "There arose not a prophet since in Israel like unto Moses, whom the LORD knew face to face" (KJV).

Then God told Moses, "Your work is now finished." Though Moses had led God's people to the border of Canaan, God wasn't going to allow him to cross over into the Promised Land. Instead, God told him, "Go up on Mount Nebo" (see Deuteronomy 32:49-52). So Moses, then 120 years old, climbed a twenty-six-hundred-foot mountain—a challenge to much younger men. Deuteronomy 34:7 tells us he was still healthy: "His eyes were not dim nor his natural vigor abated" (NKJV). But there, in obedience to God and without protest, Moses closed his eyes in death.

The apostle Paul spent the last twenty-two years of his life on three extended missionary trips, establishing new churches and writing his New Testament epistles. After that, he was thrown in prison and faced certain execution. Paul, the primary theologian of the early church, the definer of the faith, lived the faith he preached.

In a letter to the young minister Timothy, Paul wrote, "I am now ready to be offered, and the time of my departure is at hand." What were his thoughts and fears at that point of his life? He said, "I have fought a good fight, I have finished my course, I have kept the faith: Henceforth there is laid up for me a crown of righteousness, which the Lord, the righteous judge, shall give me at that day: and not to me only, but to all them that love his appearing" (2 Timothy 4:6-8, KJV).

Paul looked beyond his death. Death is only the end of life on this earth as we know it. Death is like a passageway to the fulfillment of all the Bible promises of eternal life with God. So, Paul could write, "O death, where is thy sting? O grave, where is thy victory?" (1 Corinthians 15:55). He viewed death as an event that those who believe in Christ need not fear. It had lost its power over Paul. Death can lose its power over us too.

Different philosophies

Nonbelievers may face death differently than believers do. During a smoking cessation program I held, one of the participants said he didn't believe in God or the afterlife. He added, "You probably wonder why I want to stop smoking. . . . I want to live as many years as possible." For him, life ends when we die the first death. He had no hope beyond the grave. How sad!

Even those who experience prime-time living will eventually face the "time to die." That fact we can't deny. How we face death depends on the philosophy of life by which we have lived. Let's look at three different philosophies.

The first is "I live for me. Nothing else matters. My goal is to obtain all the money I can get my hands on. The amount of my net worth is crucial, and everything else is secondary. I want to live in a mansion. I want several luxury cars, a yacht, and numerous other things that speak of prestige and power. I love myself." Death doesn't fit into this lifestyle. It ends it all.

The second philosophy is "I live for others. My goal is to help everyone I can help. I love my family. I want to make my community and world a better place. The community is my life. I'm willing to die for my country." For those with this philosophy, death is OK if it serves the right cause.

The third philosophy says, "I live for God. 'For me to live is Christ' (Philippians 1:21, KJV). 'Christ will be magnified in my body, whether by life or by death' (verse 20, NKJV). My goal is to magnify the character of God. I want to be a loving, happy, kind, and gentle person. I want to be a friend to others. Prime-time living comes naturally to me because God created my body and I believe He knows what is best for me. I want to be like Jesus and increase in wisdom, the intellectual component; in stature, the physical component; in favor with God, the spiritual component; and in favor with my fellow human beings, the social component (see Luke 2:52). In addition, I want good emotional health. God can give me all of these things and help me have a philosophy that meets His desire for my life (see Galatians 5:22, 23). I'll not worry about when I will die—that is in God's hands."

If you'll examine the way you approach life, you'll see how you're going to face death. The most revealing part of your life will be your spiritual experience. Your connection with God is more important than your intellectual achievements, your social standing, or any other area of life. If you have any doubts about the state of your spiritual health, don't delay turning to the Great Physician.

Let's enjoy prime-time aging. Let's enjoy the benefits of a quality life—physically, intellectually, emotionally, socially, and spiritually. Remember that life is measured by quality and not by quantity.

I don't know when my work on this earth will be finished. You don't know when you will complete your work. How I live my life is in my hands. I choose whether I'll live for my own enjoyment, or to benefit society, or for God, as Paul did. The time of my "departure" is in God's hands. I'll be happy to continue to live many more years on this earth if that is God's will. I'll be just as happy to finish my work here and rest, waiting to live with Christ.

Let's aim to face death as Paul did. Let's

- recognize that it is OK to die,
- live our lives so we can look back with satisfaction,
- maintain our faith in God, and
- claim the promises of eternal life with God and the home He is preparing for us.

So, don't gear down for death. Gear up to live in the new earth with God and millions of friends forever without aging. Gear up for eternal life!

★ ★ ★

I wrote this chapter from my background as a pastor and hospital chaplain. Then a routine colonoscopy revealed a tumor—cancer—in my wife, Mary-Alice. We've been married for forty-five years and have been planning for a dynamic retirement. Was I about to lose her? I was terrified.

The concepts and Bible promises in this chapter have become very personal and real to me now. They are not spiritual platitudes. By applying the chapter section entitled "Facing Our Own Death" to our situation, I was able to say, "God, I trust You completely. You know what is best for Mary-Alice. You love her, and she loves You. You have a home in heaven for her. Though I want her to live, I know You will do only what is best for her. Whatever Your will for her life, that's what I want also. Lord, she is in Your loving and almight hands."

The medical prognosis looks good, but it's iffy. However, the eternal prognosis is great—and it is certain. Our faith is strong as we face the future.—*David White*

Though I've been a vegetarian for almost forty-five years and have followed a totally plant-based diet for the past ten plus years, my family history of colorectal cancer put me at risk. (Have you had the recommended exams?) I've been through a round of chemotherapy and radiation therapy followed by surgery, from which I am recovering as I write this. The tumor was found fairly early, and the prognosis looks good.

The journey has been long, and it's not over yet. But as I face the final round of chemotherapy, I have the assurance that the Lord will continue to walk through the valley with me. I've even found joy in this difficult journey, for I've seen the Lord's name glorified as the result of my suffering, and I praise Him for this. My suffering is so miniscule compared to what He suffered for me.—*Mary-Alice White*

If you or a loved one is facing death and you're apprehensive about it, David White would be happy to talk with you. Telephone him at (863) 452-9798, or contact him through the publisher of this book.

---

1. See Elisabeth Kubler-Ross, *On Death and Dying* (New York: Scribner, 1997).

For More Information ...

Administration on Aging
(202) 619-0724
www.aoa.gov

Agency for Health Care Research & Quality
(301) 427-1364
www.ahcpr.gov

Alcoholics Anonymous
(800) 923-8722

Alzheimer's Association
(800) 272-3900
www.alz.org

American Cancer Society
(800) ACS-2345
www.cancer.org

American College of Sports Medicine
(317) 637-9200
www.acsm.org

American Council on Exercise
(800) 825-3636
www.acefitness.org

American Dental Association
(312) 440-2500
www.ada.org

American Diabetes Association
(800) DIABETES
www.diabetes.org

American Dietetic Association
(800) 877-1600
www.eatright.org

American Heart Association
(800) AHA-USA-1
www.americanheart.org

American Lung Association
(212) 315-8700
www.lungusa.org

American Stroke Association
(888) 478-7653
www.strokeassociation.org

Arthritis Foundation
(800) 568-4045
www.arthritis.org

Centers for Disease Control & Prevention
(404) 639-3311
www.cdc.gov

CDC Diabetes Home Page
(877) CDC-DIAB
www.cdcgov/diabetes

CDC National Center for Chronic Disease Prevention & Health Promotion
www.cdc.gov/nccdphp

Elderhostel
(877) 426-8056
www.elderhostel.org

Healthfinder
P.O. Box 1133
Washington, D.C. 20013-1133
(202) 205-8611
www.healthfinder.gov

National Center on Elder Abuse
(202) 898-2586
http://
www.elderabusecenter.org

National Institute of Mental Health
(866) 615-6464
www.nimh.nih.gov

National Institutes of Health
(301) 496-4000
www.nih.gov

National Osteoporosis Foundation
(800) 624-2663; (202) 223-2226
www.nof.org

National Sleep Foundation
(202) 347-3471
www.sleepfoundation.org

National Stroke Association
(800) STROKES
www.stroke.org

NIH National Institute on Aging
(800) 222-2225
www.nih.gov/nia

Office of Disease Prevention & Health Promotion
(240) 453-8280
www.odphp.osophs.dhhs.gov

Tufts Nutrition
(617) 636-3736
http://nutrition.tufts.edu

Veterans Affairs Office
(800) 827-1000
www.va.gov

If you enjoyed this book, you'll enjoy these as well:

Defeating Diabetes
Brenda Davis Vesanto Melina
Defeating Diabetes gives real solutions for people with adult onset (Type II) diabetes. Includes lists of foods that help overcome insulin resistance, a self-care checklist for physical and emotional well-being, more than 50 recipes with menus, and information on alternative and conventional therapies.
1-5706-7139-7. Paperback.
US$14.95, Can$20.45.

The Seventh-day Diet
Chris Rucker
This helpful book provides a practical plan to apply the Adventist lifestyle. Includes dozens of natural foods recipes, a personal exercise program, weight-loss principles, and more.
0-8163-1868-9. Paperback.
US$14.99 Can$20.49.

Dr. Arnott's 24 Realistic Ways to Improve Your Health
Tim Arnott, MD of the Lifestyle Center of America has produced this helpful book of short, practical suggestions based on scientific research and a Bible-based lifestyle. Following his advice will help you live longer, happier, and more healthfully!
0-8163-2029-2. Paper.
US$1.99, Can$2.69.

Order from your ABC by calling **1-800-765-6955,** or get online and shop our virtual store at **www.AdventistBookCenter.com.**
• Read a chapter from your favorite book
• Order online
• Sign up for email notices on new products

Prices subject to change without notice.